FRANKFURT

CONDENSED

angela cullen

LONELY PLANET PUBLICATIONS
Melbourne • Oakland • London • Paris

contents

Frankfurt Condensed
1st edition – September 2000

Published by
Lonely Planet Publications Pty Ltd
ABN 36 005 607 983
192 Burwood Rd, Hawthorn,
Victoria 3122, Australia

Lonely Planet Offices
Australia PO Box 617, Hawthorn, VIC 3122
USA 150 Linden St, Oakland, CA 94607
UK 10a Spring Place, London NW5 3BH
France 1 rue du Dahomey, 75011 Paris

Photographs
All of the images in this guide are available for licensing from Lonely Planet Images.
email: lpi@lonelyplanet.com.au

Front cover photographs
Top: Frankfurt skyline (Martin Moos)
Bottom: The *Hammering Man* sculpture at the trade fair grounds (Charlotte Hindle)

ISBN 1 86450 223 1

Printed by Colorcraft Ltd, Hong Kong

how to use this book

KEY TO SYMBOLS

- address
- telephone number
- email/web site address
- nearest U-bahn or S-bahn station
- nearest tram route
- nearest bus route
- nearest train station
- airport
- tourist information
- opening hours
- cost, entry charge
- wheelchair access
- child-friendly
- on-site or nearby eatery
- vegetarian, or includes vegetarian options

COLOUR-CODING

Each chapter has a different colour code which is reflected on the maps for quick reference (eg all Highlights are bright yellow on the maps).

MAPS & GRID REFERENCES

The fold-out maps on the front and back covers are numbered from 1 to 5. All sights and venues in the text have map references which indicate where to find them; eg, (2, G5) means Map 2, grid reference G5. All sights and many other items are marked on the maps. For items not marked, the street is marked.

PRICES

Price gradings (eg DM10/6) usually indicate adult/concession entry charges. Concession prices can include child, pensioner and/or student discounts, and most attractions offer them. Where only 1 price (adult) is listed, there will generally still be concession rates available.

WARNING & REQUEST

Things change – prices go up, schedules change, good places go bad and bad places improve or go bankrupt. So, if you find things better or worse, recently opened or long since closed, please tell us and help make the next edition even more accurate. Everyone who writes to us will find their name and possibly excerpts from their correspondence in one of our publications (let us know if you *don't* want your letter published or your name acknowledged). They will also receive the latest issue of *Planet Talk*, our quarterly printed newsletter, or *Comet*, our monthly email newsletter. Subscriptions to both newsletters are free. The very best contributions will be rewarded with a free guidebook.

Send all correspondence to the Lonely Planet office closest to you (p. 123).

Lonely Planet books provide independent advice. Lonely Planet does not accept advertising in guidebooks, nor payment in exchange for listing or endorsing any place or business. Lonely Planet writers do not accept discounts or payments in exchange for positive coverage of any sort.

facts about frankfurt

Forget the flair of Hamburg and the majesty of Munich. As for the party towns Cologne and Berlin, leave them to it. Frankfurt may be smaller and less flamboyant than its siblings, but it stands head and shoulders above them. Not only because it boasts Germany's most spectacular skyline and Europe's tallest office building, but also because it's the country's most international town: more than a quarter of its citizens are foreign, making it one of Germany's most tolerant cities.

In many ways, Frankfurt is the German capital that never was. It was the cradle of German democracy, a major European trade centre for nearly 1000 years, and, after WWII, almost became the capital. Its airport is the largest in Europe after Heathrow. It's also Continental Europe's financial capital, home to one of the world's largest banks, and has the world's 4th largest stock exchange. It's a city on the move.

Still, in its heart, it's a city of villages. Critics say this makes it too provincial to cope with the global challenge; fans say its homespun flavour and compact size add to its character and liveableness. There's no denying it's a city that has to be discovered; it doesn't invite you in. The lack of a true centre for its thriving nightlife and countless eateries means many of the city's offerings remain insider tips, which thankfully also preserves their charm. While it brags about its modern architectural assets and its banking prowess, it's shy to reveal its true persona as a lover of the arts and a hive of multicultural activity.

The main reason for these anomalies is that Frankfurt is reinventing itself. The town that was buried beneath the rubble of WWII bombing became a permanent building site, and it's still not clear what the finished product will look like. Frankfurt wouldn't win any beauty contests. Nor does it try to hide its past. But it's forging ahead, scars and all. And the world capital that's emerging is definitely worth the visit – it won't leave you wanting.

Martin Moos

Bridges across the Main River, linking the two halves of Frankfurt

HISTORY

Celtic and Roman remains show that the area's first settlers knew a good spot when they saw it, long before the name Frankfurt appeared on the map. Römerstadt, on the northern boundary of today's city, was as big as medieval Frankfurt, but existed 700 years before the first references to Franconofurd appeared in 794. The Frankish king Charlemagne liked the place so much he promoted it to one of his royal residences, but he had a job keeping the warring Franks and Saxons apart on either side of the river. Even today, the citizens of Sachsenhausen are adamant that they are *Sachsenhäuser* first, Frankfurters second.

Election & Coronation Capital

Frederick I (Barbarossa) was elected the first German emperor in Frankfurt in 1152, as the city grew in political importance. Frankfurt became the electoral, and later the coronation, capital, with a total of 10 emperors crowned here.

The city also gained in prominence as a trade centre. By the 14th century, Frankfurt hosted 2 thriving international trade fairs. And even then Frankfurters were displaying their strong will and fierce independence. In 1372 they bought their autonomy from Karl IV for 8800 Gulden, making Frankfurt a *freie Reichsstadt*, or free imperial city.

Frankfurt's Jews

While Frankfurters are generally liberal and tolerant, moments in history show they weren't always that way. As Christians across Europe began imposing restrictions on Jews, Frankfurt also wielded its strong arm. In the 15th century, it banished its 3000 Jewish citizens to a ghetto at Börneplatz. The ghetto was bombarded by the French in 1796, scattering the Jews across the city.

The 19th century fight for civic liberties raised their status for a while, before anti-Semitism returned with a vengeance, almost wiping out a Jewish community that gave Frankfurt its banking tradition, and much of its academic and cultural heritage. Of the 30,000 Jews that lived in Frankfurt before the 1933 pogrom, 10,000 were deported and murdered, while others fled.

Anne Frank was one who escaped to Amsterdam with her family, where they were captured by the Gestapo in 1944. She perished at Bergen-Belsen a few months later.

Oskar Schindler, a German who saved over 1000 Jews from the gas chambers, died a poor man in Frankfurt.

From Occupation to Revolution

Frankfurt was a refuge for many Dutch and French fleeing religious persecution in the 16th and 17th centuries, but was itself invaded by Swedish troops in 1631 during the Thirty Years' War. In 1759-63 French troops occupied the city during the Seven Years' War, and again at the turn of the 18th century during the Napoleonic Wars.

The peasant revolt that engulfed Europe in the early 19th century led to a brief, heroic German uprising in 1848. This spawned a fledgling democracy and the country's first freely elected national assembly, which convened in Frankfurt, of all places. But the revolution was crushed after just 14 months.

World Wars & Revival

As with the rest of Germany, two world wars left their impact. Many Frankfurters were evacuated to the outlying regions during WWII. Over 800 Allied bombing raids in one night in 1944 left 1870 people dead and the city centre in ruins. The American army liberated the city in 1945 and used it as their headquarters during Germany's rehabilitation. It was here that the Deutschmark was born, driving the postwar economic recovery.

Frankfurters embraced American culture, so much so that it's dubbed Germany's most American town. Nonetheless, in the 60s and 70s Frankfurters staged demonstrations against US involvement in Vietnam.

Golden Years

As the German economy sailed through the oil crises and recessions that rattled the rest of the world, Frankfurt – as the seat of the Deutsche Bundesbank – took its place at the country's financial helm. Following unification in 1990, Frankfurt am Main was reunited with its eastern namesake, Frankfurt an der Oder.

The expansion of Frankfurt airport into Continental Europe's largest has had no mean role in the city's growth and international standing. This was a factor in it being chosen over London as the seat of the European Central Bank, a mantle it's beginning to wear with confidence. It was here that the new euro currency was launched on 1 January 1999.

Frankfurt also owes much of its international recognition to its trade fairs, which attract millions of visitors every year.

Frankfurt Today & Tomorrow

Frankfurt has risen from the ashes, but knows it can't stand still. With the 298m Commerzbank building leading the skyscraper charge, the skyline is expanding, and plans are afoot to revive the river banks and the eyesore between the trade fair centre and main train station.

The airport is expanding at an alarming rate, and Frankfurt has become the fulcrum for Germany's rail network. Locals may grumble about the heartless face of big business, but they're secretly proud of Frankfurt's world recognition.

Of course, all this has its price. Frankfurt is Germany's most expensive city. But it's cheap at twice the price compared with Paris or London. And a lot easier to navigate.

Martin Moos

The Deutsche Bank's soaring glass towers

ORIENTATION

All roads lead to Frankfurt. Well, maybe not all, but most of Germany's *Autobahnen* converge at Frankfurt. It's neatly pocketed in a valley below the northern Taunus Hills, equidistant from Hamburg and the Alps.

Frankfurt covers 249 sq km at the centre of the greater Rhine-Main region. The Main and Rhine Rivers meet at the town of Mainz, 40km west of Frankfurt.

The Main River (pronounced 'mine') traverses Frankfurt east-west. South of the river, Sachsenhausen is a self-contained town within a town, with a jumbled mix of shops, restaurants, bars and museums. The student district of Bockenheim in the north-west rubs shoulders with the well-heeled Westend, while neighbouring Nordend and Bornheim carry the bohemian flag. A few good eateries don't save the Bahnhofsviertel around the main train station from remaining a seedy red-light district. The Ostend is an up-and-coming hub for nightlife and the alternative scene.

The outlying towns of Bad Homburg, Kronberg and Königstein are the province of wealthy bank directors and speculators.

Modern and traditional architecture merge at the trade fair centre.

ENVIRONMENT

Germans are the world's greatest separators when it comes to garbage. The country that gave the world bottle banks also invented the organic trash can, and probably any other type of garbage can imaginable. Frankfurters have figured out how to make money from being environmentally conscious, which explains why refuse collection prices have gone through the roof since the city's waste department was privatised a few years ago.

Traffic gets heavy at rush hour (7-9am, 4.30-7pm), but smog alerts are few and far between. Pollen can be troublesome, however, due to the city's inland location. This also makes Frankfurt susceptible to sudden temperature changes as hot and cold weather fronts fight it out in the skies above.

Outbreaks of graffiti create the impression Frankfurt is unclean, but on closer inspection its streets and parks are no dirtier than any other German city.

GOVERNMENT & POLITICS

Although Frankfurt missed the boat when they were selecting capital cities, and it doesn't play a role in federal politics, it's still Germany's most important city economically. Monetarists and influential bankers meet here to decide interest rates and money supply for the entire euro-zone. It's the seat of the European Central Bank and headquarters to Deutsche Bank, one of the world's largest asset management banks and the unofficial manager of the German economy.

Political Persuasion

Frankfurt was nearly chosen as Germany's capital after WWII, but the first federal chancellor, Konrad Adenauer, swayed the vote in favour of Bonn – it was closer to his home. Frankfurters had been so confident of becoming the administrative capital they had begun building a parliament before the vote was taken; the round-shaped Goldhalle was later transformed into a radio studio.

Despite its capitalist leanings, Frankfurt was ruled from 1989 by the leftist Social Democrats (SPD) and the Green Party. They were instrumental in attacking Frankfurt's drug problem, an all-too-evident facet of big-city life, and confronting the growth of homelessness.

Municipal elections in 1997 failed to produce a ruling majority, resulting in a grand coalition between the rightist Christian Democrat Party (CDU) and the Social Democrats at the time of writing. Their ideological differences often cause a log jam in policy-making. The Green Party was ousted from government.

The mayor is directly elected by the people, and presides over the municipal parliament of 93 members.

ECONOMY

Frankfurt is one of Germany's richest cities, although only its 5th largest. Some 240 foreign banks are represented here with an annual business volume of DM3.3 billion. Over DM8 trillion changes hands on the Frankfurt stock exchange every year. While shifting towards a services-based economy – it's a magnet for biotech, design, software, advertising, film and multimedia companies – Frankfurt has a deep-rooted industrial tradition in chemicals, cars and machinery.

Frankfurt Figures

Unemployment	under 10%
GDP	DM90 billion
Flight passengers per year	44 million
Foreign banks	240
Museums	40
City parks	48
Theatres	33
Price of 125 sq m apartment	DM750,000
Average price of double hotel room	DM200

Frankfurt airport, as the hub of Continental Europe's air traffic, is probably the only reason many people have heard of Frankfurt – it's also the region's largest single employment centre. It is a factor in Frankfurt's prominence as an international trade fair centre.

SOCIETY & CULTURE

Labourers from Turkey, Greece, Spain and Italy were invited to help rebuild Germany in the 1950s and 60s. Frankfurt, with its easy airport access, was the first port of call for many. While there is little sign of cultural intolerance in Frankfurt, many first-generation immigrants resist integration, and the same could be said about Frankfurt's latest wave of 'guest workers', the highly transient expat community. But for many Frankfurters as for many western Germans, the greatest cultural hurdle lies at their own front door: accepting their eastern German siblings. Still, Frankfurters are extremely receptive to other cultures, especially Anglo-Saxon.

With a population of 650,000, Frankfurt is home to around 50,000 former Yugoslavs, 40,000 Italians and Spanish, respectively, 36,000 Turks, 20,000 Americans, 12,000 French and British, and 4000 Japanese and Koreans. Travelling around the city, you'll find German is often the last language heard. English is the language of business and is spoken well by most young Germans.

Character & Etiquette

Like Germans elsewhere, Frankfurters are an honest bunch, so honest that when you go into a bar, you immediately get a tab. They have a no-nonsense attitude to life, and aren't afraid to speak their mind, which often leads to lively public discourse. Hardly a day goes by without a public demonstration decrying some injustice. Frankfurters like people to believe they carry the world on their shoulders, but really it's just an excuse to display their underdog sense of humour. They don't suffer fools gladly. They may come across as gruff, but this is just their way of showing that no-one should expect special treatment, not even newcomers to the city. They're tolerant and have a live-and-let-live philosophy to life.

Dos & Don'ts

Expect to be publicly reprimanded for jaywalking, a finable offence. Queues form democratically, and queue-hoppers will be demonstratively reminded of their fault. Smoking is prohibited in subways and public buildings, but otherwise Frankfurt is a smokers' paradise.

Martin Moos

'OK, who ordered the vegetarian Frankfurters?'

ARTS

Literature

Not to mention Frankfurt's literary son, Johann Wolfgang von Goethe, would be a serious omission, even if Germany's equivalent of Shakespeare allegedly hated the place. Goethe's relationship with his home town was a fiery one. The city never forgave the writer-cum-philosopher for reneging his citizenship of Frankfurt and denying the city coffers valuable taxes. But Goethe visited Frankfurt frequently after he moved away, so it can't have been that disagreeable to him.

Angela Cullen

Goethe, Germany's leading literary figure

The Frankfurt Book Fair has become a fixed date in the world's literary calendar, attracting around a quarter of a million visitors (see Trade Fairs, p. 13). Frankfurt is also a major publishing capital with over 500 publishing houses and affiliates.

Performing Arts

In the 1980s New Yorker William Forsythe initiated Frankfurters into the world of modern ballet. He started a troupe known as the Frankfurt Ballet, which didn't always enjoy the cult status it has today. Once dismayed at the disjointed movements and harsh sounds that went under the name of ballet, Frankfurters now join in the scramble for tickets as the ballet performs to a permanently full house.

The former soap factory Mousonturm draws travelling dance groups and performance artists from around the world, with the emphasis on the experimental. Das TAT in the Bockenheimer Depot is the pre-eminent avant-garde performance art venue in Europe.

First Call

The telephone was invented in Frankfurt – unfortunately nobody took notice at the time, despite inventor Philipp Reis' best efforts to convince people of the viability of his prototype. Three years after his death in 1874, Germany's first telephone connection was introduced and Reis' next of kin were awarded an annual pension of 1000 marks.

Music

Frankfurt has been at the forefront of Germany's music scene. While local artists such as Sven Väth and DJ Talla spawned the European techno revolution in the mid-80s, jazz expert Albert Mangelsdorff still captivates audiences 50 years on. Composer Paul Hindemith is a celebrated son. The progressive Ensemble Modern gives regular

Hot Jazz

In the late 1930s, local musicians risked their lives to foster a jazz scene that lives on today. Back then, the Nazis outlawed all forms of 'degenerate' art. The Mangelsdorff brothers were members of the secret Harlem Club, where they met to play their illicit melodies. Not surprisingly, the 50s was a decade of celebration as world stars such as Dizzy Gillespie, Eddie Harris and Louis Armstrong visited Frankfurt.

Martin Moos

concerts at the Alte Oper, and orchestras such as the Viennese Philharmonic and The Academy of St Martin in the Fields visit regularly.

There is no shortage of live music gigs, opera, classical, rock and pop concerts, as well as a healthy subterranean party scene. Around March annually, Frankfurt stages the International Music Trade Fair, attracting musicians from all over the world. The International Jazz Festival is also a major musical event.

Painting

Frankfurt's rich painting tradition couldn't have flowered without the help of Johann Friedrich Städel. This propertied 18th-century luminary launched the Städel foundation and bequeathed his art collection to the city; the Städel Art Institute has a world-class collection of works.

Expressionist Max Beckmann came to Frankfurt in 1918 to visit, but ended up staying 15 years before fleeing from the Nazis. His paintings of the Eiserner Steg footbridge and The Synagogue hang in the Städel, where he taught budding artists for many years.

Film

The only film-maker of international fame to come from the region is Volker Schlöndorff, who hails from Wiesbaden. Frankfurt is more noted for its postproduction prowess than film direction, but is home to the German Film Museum and the country's most extensive film archive.

Philosophy & Architecture

Frankfurters have made their mark in the worlds of philosophy and architecture. At the Institute for Social Research, the Frankfurt School, including Max Horkheimer and Theodor Adorno, developed their radical Marxist social theory.

Architect and town planner Ernst May took Bauhaus a step further by conceiving a series of satellite housing projects which also contain the revolutionary *Frankfurter Bad* (bathroom) and the *Frankfurter Küche* (kitchen).

TRADE FAIRS

The world flocks to Frankfurt for its trade fairs – 3 million-odd visitors each year, in fact. The city has a long history, dating from the 13th century, of hosting trade fairs, thanks to its position at the hub of Europe's main trade routes. From textiles, music and the meat industry to the massive IAA international motor show (over 1 million visitors) and the largest book fair in the world, the vast array of fairs has seen a huge self-contained complex of exhibition halls (the *Messe*) develop, centred around the 1909 Festhalle. Helmut Jahn's 256m-high Messeturm was the tallest office block in Europe when built in 1988-91.

March to May and September/October are usually the busiest times of year for the Messe, and when hotel rooms are scarcest.

For further details check out the Messe's Web site at www.messefrankfurt.com or email info@messefrankfurt.com. Map 4 depicts the Messe district.

Frankfurt Book Fair

Although it has become as much a multimedia exhibition as a platform for publishers, the Frankfurt Book Fair is where, once a year, the world's publishing industry gets together. Usually held in October, it attracts over a quarter of a million visitors to examine the wares of nearly 7000 exhibitors. Titles are bought and sold, licensing, copyright and distribution deals are struck, 'dummy' books are tested out and ideas are hatched. The fair is open to the public on the last 2 days only.

Trade Fair Survival Tips

- Come 1 or 2 days early if you want to have any time for sightseeing.
- Book restaurants for client dinners well in advance. The ones near the Messe fill up early. As it's almost impossible to get a taxi after the fair has closed, choose evening entertainment either within walking distance of the fair or near a train/tram stop.
- Accommodation also needs to be organised well in advance. Obtaining a good, centrally located hotel room is very difficult, and rooms in the best hotels are often booked years in advance.
- Catering at the fair is pretty dismal, and it's also difficult to leave your stand in order to buy or eat food. A good tip is to take some sandwiches into the fair with you.
- Get used to cigarette smoke – the fair is a smokers' paradise and hell for nonsmokers.
- Don't check in late for your flight to Frankfurt. While airlines routinely overbook, expecting an average 10% no-show rate, when it's fair time the no-show rate is negligible – so passengers get bumped to a later flight.

Charlotte Hindle

Congress Centre and Messeturm

highlights

Frankfurt is best viewed on foot. Most of its obvious attractions are located around the city centre. It's an outdoor city that shows its best side from May to October. From world-renowned galleries and green oases to bohemian districts and medieval townships, the selection of highlights here is a tossed salad of regular greens and some tasty, unexpected morsels that offer a glimpse of Frankfurt's contrasts and quirks.

Great Views

- a boat ride on the Main (p. 54) for the best view of the skyline
- the 590m-high Lohrberg hill top (p. 20), the highest vantage point within the city limits
- the rotating restaurant atop the Henninger brewery building (p. 81), for the changing scenery
- the viewing gallery at the top of the Main Tower office block

Martin Moos

City skyline across the Main River

Stopping Over?

One Day Hop on the Applewine Express tram for a kitschy 1hr ride around the highlights and lowlights. Pick a spot on the south river bank and watch the world and his dog go by before heading for the lively Sachsenhausen district to sample the local juice and victuals (a rare blend of acid and stodge).

Two Days Visit one of the many museums dotted around the river embankment. Wait till dark before heading for the 200m-high viewing gallery atop the Main Tower for a night view of the impressive skyline. Move on to the Hanauer Landstrasse, the hub of Frankfurt's most interesting and offbeat nightlife.

Three Days Join the thousands of in-line skaters who speed through the city with police escort every Tuesday night (p. 44) for a non-biased view of Frankfurt and its districts. Round off with beers and top-notch pub grub in Nordend or Bockenheim.

Frankfurt Lowlights

Bahnhofsviertel The main train station was Europe's largest building when built in 1888, and the Kaiserstrasse a promenade of bourgeois town houses. Now the area is a seedy, drug-ridden, red-light district trying desperately to dress itself up with theatre, nightclubs and eateries. The Reeperbahn it's not.

Main River Once 'Frankfurt's Nice', the now-shabby Main River embankment was a place to see and be seen in the 1930s, decked with swimming pools and palm trees. While moves are afoot to restore the river banks, they still have a way to go before they regain their former glory.

BOCKENHEIM (1, D3)

Of all Frankfurt's districts, Bockenheim is the most laid-back. It's a hive of cafes, bars, quirky shops and restaurants for every palate. Try Celsius on Leipziger Strasse for a tapas platter to die for, while Andalucia and Abendmahl are the hot tips on Konrad-Brosswitz-Strasse.

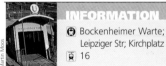

Take a walk down cobblestoned Leipziger Strasse on Saturday at noon to capture the lively atmosphere of Bockenheim. There's a familiarity in the air, and a sense of people with a purpose. This is multicultural Frankfurt at its best.

Martin Moos

INFORMATION

- Bockenheimer Warte; Leipziger Str; Kirchplatz
- 16

The **Leipziger Markt**, at 2 locations along the street, is an excellent Turkish fresh fruit and vegetable market, whose owners can be heard as far away as the Bockenheimer Warte!

One of 4 watchtowers erected in the 15th century to guard the city, the **Bockenheimer Warte** (4, A5) doubled as a windmill in the 1600s and these days serves as a ventilation facility for the sewerage system. The Thursday **market** (8am-6pm) here is a big attraction. **Das TAT** (4, A5; p. 96), the renowned centre for the performing arts, is in a disused train depot opposite; the Frankfurt Ballet also performs here.

From the stone-fired pizzas at fast-food Italian places on Adalbertstrasse to brunch specialist Albatross and the 20-year-old Ulli's Backstube cafe at the university, the old familiars are the rule rather than the exception in Bockenheim. But new additions like the modern Cafe Klemm on Kiesstrasse also have their place.

Don't forget Schlossstrasse, home to the wine cellar and live jazz venue La Bohème, the Bockenheimer Weinkontor with a wine list as long as a stalk of vine, and the British/Irish pub restaurant Castle Inn.

Charlotte Hindle

The Gothic Bockenheimer Warte

DON'T MISS

- Quartier Latin, the university's answer to Mardi Gras, an all-night fancy dress ball held in February or March each year

BORNHEIM (1, D9)

Berger Strasse is the spinal cord of the district of Bornheim, the traditional working class part of town. These days, it prefers the label 'bohemian', an image it measures up to well with its mix of dusty bookstores, health food shops and inexpensive restaurants.

INFORMATION

- Bornheim Mitte; Höhenstr; Merianplatz
- 12

Cosy dining at Weisse Lilie restaurant (p.75)

The **Berger Kinos** movie theatre at the Uhrtürmchen, or clock tower, is always good for an offbeat movie (but not always in English), and the Saturday open-air **food market** there is the best of an excellent bunch around the city. Bornheim is known locally as 'the jolly village', and it shows.

As you walk north, **Upper Berger Strasse** has its magic moments, with Weisse Lilie, a bustling restaurant with a Spanish bent, and Zur Sonne, a gigantic summer garden restaurant that holds hundreds. The live music venue Blues & Beyond may have a sterile decor, but concerts held there are full of personality.

Lower Berger Strasse (1, E8), which is also claimed by Nordenders and even some Ostenders, at a stretch, has sold its soul to yuppiedom but has managed to escape with no bad after-taste. The sound of chatter on its endless row of cafes coaxes people out of the woodwork like the strains of a Schubert serenade on a summer evening. A Spanish Rioja at cafe/bookshop Ypsilon is the perfect way to end the day.

Play chess at the giant board set in the tranquil **Bethmann Park** (2, C10; p. 39), or watch old men playing *boules* in a distant corner. The walled Chinese garden inside this peaceful park at the bottom of Berger Strasse was created in 1990 in memory of the victims of the Tiananmen Square massacre.

DON'T MISS

- smelling and sampling the coffee at Wacker
- Wed and Sat night jazz session in the tiny Mampf, on Sandweg
- sighting a grey heron in the Friedberger Anlage pond

FRANKFURT AIRPORT (5, C6)

Airports aren't generally the kind of place to do sightseeing, but tell that to the hundreds of Frankfurt families who head out to Europe's 2nd-largest airport at weekends to watch planes from the viewing galleries. Apart from plane-spotting (well over 1000 planes take off and land every day), there are many other airport attractions a mere 15-minute subway ride from the city centre.

The Airport Gallery in Hall B hosts regular art exhibitions as well as two of the best Easter and Christmas markets around for handcrafts. Terminal 1 also offers good shopping in the shape of Parisian and Italian fashions, top-rate leather goods, and expensive cosmetics and perfume – even a Harrod's outlet and a Body Shop. And techno fans gravitate from all over the region to the Dorian Gray nightclub (or rather all-day-all-night club as revellers pile out late on Sunday mornings).

The futuristic Terminal 2 was added in 1996, and also has a viewing gallery and art exhibition space as well as a kiddies' amusement area. It's more relaxed than the frenzied Terminal 1, although shopping and leisure amenities aren't as plentiful. Its strong glass-and-ribbing structure makes it stand out starkly against the night sky.

Undergoing construction near the site of the Terminal 2 building is the state-of-the-art AIRail Terminal, which has already begun to link up to the interregional rail network. This will gradually become the hub for Germany's high-speed ICE rail network.

Chris Mellor

INFORMATION

- ✉ 10km southwest of city centre
- Ⓤ Flughafen
- ☎ 69 07 02 91/92 (airport info), 69 03 05 11 (flight info); see also p. 108
- e www.frankfurt-airport.de
- ♿ good

Airport Tours

A visitors' service organises tours around the airport for groups of 20 or more (☎ 702 91/92), and there are also public tours available at various times that can be joined by individuals without a reservation. The visitors' terraces are open daily 8am-7.30pm (☎ 69 07 00 69).

Martin Moos

Frankfurt Airport, a bustling city within a city

GOETHE-HAUS & GOETHEMUSEUM (2, G6)

This was Goethe's parents' house, and is a wonderful example of how Frankfurt's well-to-do lived in the 18th century. It was here that Goethe was born in 1749 and lived until moving to Weimar in 1775, an act that many Frankfurters found hard to forgive him for even though he often wrote of his fondness for the town. It's also one of the most visited spots on the cultural trail, so choose your moment if you want to browse around at leisure.

Of the 2 timber-framed houses, the Goethe-Haus will probably take up more of your time than the museum, filled as it is with the charms of a real family home as it was more than 250 years ago. The museum contains a library of the writer's works.

Leading into the little garden between the museum and the Goethe-Haus, the rococo anteroom with wall paintings by Johann Conrad Seekatz depicting the months of the year has an interesting story to tell: so taken was he with Goethe senior's art collection, the French lieutenant Francois Théas Comte de Thoranc had many of the paintings spirited away to his residence in the south of France after occupying the house during the Seven Years' War. Many were rediscovered in France in the 19th century and returned, including Seekatz's renditions.

The Goethe-Haus was reconstructed in 1951 after war damage, and it and the adjoining Goethemuseum underwent a major facelift in the mid-1990s. Tours in English can be organised in advance.

INFORMATION

- ✉ Grosser Hirschgraben 23-25
- ☎ 13 88 00
- Hauptwache; Willy-Brandt-Platz
- 11
- Mon-Fri 9am-6pm (Oct-Mar to 4pm), Sat-Sun 10am-4pm
- $ DM7
- ♿ facilities in museum only

Angela Cullen

Martin Moos

Goethe-Haus, where 'Faust' was begun

DON'T MISS

- fine coffee, wine or bistro fare at Dichtung & Wahrheit (Am Salzhaus)
- the exquisite garden between the museum building & the main house

HÖCHST (5, C6)

There are plenty of places in Frankfurt to get away from it all, but the township of Höchst is a charming attraction. This medieval town boomed in the 18th century with the development of housing projects for the employees at the porcelain factory Höchster Porzellan, and later the chemical conglomerate Farbwerke Hoechst.

Architecturally, it's one of the most interesting parts of Frankfurt. The baroque **Bolongaro Palast** (1780), the **Höchster Schloss** and the wonderfully intact timber-housed old town, built between the 15th and 19th centuries, are in stark contrast to the shiver-inducing expressionist **Behrens building** (p. 32) in the industrial park. Another attraction is the **museum** of Höchst Porcelain (p. 36).

Martin Moos

INFORMATION

- ✉ 10km from city centre
- Ⓢ Höchst
- 🚊 10, 11

Martin Moos

Traditional estate house in Höchst

Höchst's traditional working-class community has been joined in recent decades by a growing immigrant population, making the town even more multicultural than Frankfurt itself. There is an enviable community spirit, as the energetic street festivals and markets attest, and cultural offerings range from slapstick theatre to high-class dance acts like the Hubbard Street Dance group and classical concerts at the **Jahrhunderthalle**.

Martin Moos

The magnificent Bolongaro Palast

There is nowhere more glorious to enjoy an applewine and a Schnitzel than at an outdoor restaurant in the cobblestoned **Marktplatz**. Many cyclists find their way out here.

The hotel boat Hotelschiff Peter Schlott anchored on the Main provides an interesting alternative to the overpriced hotels in the city. And the Neues Theater Höchst and Cafe Wunderbar on Antoniterstrasse prove that in the nightlife stakes, Höchst has what it takes to contribute to Frankfurt's cosmopolitan streak. The Neues Theater is a cabaret-cum-comedy club with regular acts from Britain, and Wunderbar is a happening bistro-bar with quirky restrooms and changing art exhibitions.

LOHRBERG (1, A11)

If the walk up the steep and narrow path from the north-eastern suburb of Seckbach doesn't kill you, the panorama from the Lohrberg might just take whatever breath is left in your lungs and finish you off.

INFORMATION

✉ Auf dem Lohr, Seckbach

🚌 43

Martin Moos

Martin Moos

A Lohrberg walking path overlooking the city skyline

Scanning due south, the factories and tower blocks of the town of Offenbach are framed by the forested hills of the Odenwald way off in the distance. As you turn westwards, the smell of beer brewing at the Henninger Turm wafts almost all the way from the hill over Sachsenhausen, before the Frankfurt skyline and the Taunus Hills hove into view. From this 590m vantage point, the entire Rhine-Main region ebbs and flows in a tide of green and concrete.

People flock here to laze on the grassy verges, grill steaks, play volleyball or ramble through the perfectly manicured **garden allotments** unique to Frankfurt.

There's a paddle pool for kiddies up to the age of 12, and a playground. On the steep hillside below is Frankfurt's only **vineyard**, which produces up to 8000 bottles of white wine a year. These are stored at the Römer and used for official ceremonies.

The **Beratergarten** to the east behind the vineyard is an experimental orchard, maintained by the city, where visitors can take a guided tour and receive gardening tips.

In winter, try **sledding** on the marked out Rodelbahn stretch (at your own risk).

For sustenance, or simply a refreshing applewine or Löwenbräu beer, pay a visit to the Lohrberg Schänke beer garden. The old men in waistcoats are some of the most entertaining waiting staff you'll meet in Frankfurt.

Schrebergärten

You'll notice on the outskirts of Frankfurt collections of garden allotments that some tourists have mistaken for extremely well kept slums! These so-called *Schrebergärten* are in fact gardens rented by Frankfurters who live in high-rise apartment blocks and built-up streets. This is where they can grow more than just a few balcony plants. You can walk around and view the allotments at the Lohrberg. Others are located at Ziegelhüttenweg in Sachsenhausen.

MUSEUM FÜR MODERNE KUNST (3, B3)

The Museum of Modern Art occupies an odd-shaped building that Austrian architect Hans Hollein designed. Inside, a labyrinth of passages leads you round the bright, white and multicoloured exhibition rooms of all shapes and sizes. American art of the 1960s and 70s meets its trans-Atlantic counterpart, with giant Roy Lichtensteins and Andy Warhols juxtaposed against European artworks. Take your time – it's impossible to hurry around, and too intriguing. View the exhibits from odd angles, from tiny, elevated viewing balconies or unobtrusive side entrances. Some are hidden in narrow stairwells and cubbyholes, others fill a whole wall. This is the most challenging and provocative contribution to Frankfurt's 'Museums Mile'.

Martin Moos

INFORMATION

- ✉ Domstr 10
- ☎ 21 23 04 47
- Römer
- 11
- Tues-Sun 10am-5pm (Wed to 8pm)
- $ DM10
- www.frankfurt-business.de/mmk
- ♿ excellent

NATURMUSEUM SENCKENBERG (4, B4)

This is Frankfurt's busiest museum and is especially popular among the young folk. The excited chatter that fills the air makes a welcome change from the whispers of other museums. From mummified cats to the anaconda swallowing a water boar, and human remains dating back thousands of years, there's enough material for a 2nd and a 3rd visit.

But it's the dinosaur bones that draw the biggest gasps, as these giant remains of the one-time rulers of the earth stand commandingly 10 and 20 times higher than the visitors gawking up at them. The development of this museum and the world-acclaimed Senckenberg research institute was enabled by the forward-thinking Frankfurt academic and medical doctor Johann Christian Senckenberg, who set up his research foundation in 1763.

Angela Cullen

INFORMATION

- ✉ Senckenberganlage 25, Bockenheim
- ☎ 754 20
- Bockenheimer Warte
- 16, 19
- 32
- 9am-5pm (Wed to 8pm, Sat-Sun to 6pm)
- $ DM7
- www.senckenberg.uni-frankfurt.de
- ♿ excellent

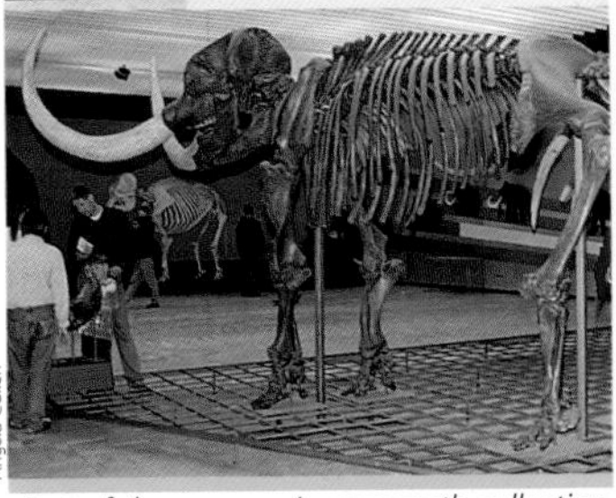

Angela Cullen

Part of the museum's mammoth collection

NORDEND (1, D7)

Finding your way around Nordend is like fumbling for a light switch in the dark. This sprawling mass roughly spans the area between Friedberger Landstrasse and Eschersheimer Landstrasse and, with more than 57,000 inhabitants, is Frankfurt's most populous district.

And it contains some of Frankfurt's best-kept secrets: the diminutive **Holzhausen Park** and moated baroque castle, the **Holzhausenschlösschen**, which hosts literary evenings and exhibitions; the **Deutsche Bibliothek**, Germany's national library (1, C7), looking like a ship about to set sail, that contains original copies of all the country's publications since 1913; and the **Hauptfriedhof** cemetery (1, C8), where some of Frankfurt's most famous thinkers and writers now rest.

It's an affluent part of town as the carefully manicured gardens and rich, century-old houses and villas reveal. The best way to appreciate Nordend is to get lost in it. Then you might happen to fall into Molly's bar/restaurant, a wonderful discovery on Spohrstrasse, or the youthful Cafe 5 in an old bunker at Glauburgstrasse.

You'll hear the crowds in Grössenwahn before you see them, which tells you just how popular this colourful meeting point is. And then there's the delightful 'living room' bar at Werkstatt Kino Mal Seh'n on Adlerflychtstrasse which also has a tiny movie theatre that shows old classics, European art-house films, and Emma Peel productions.

Check out Stalburg, at Glauburgstrasse 80, a baroque town house once surrounded by a moat and now housing a pub-restaurant and theatre that serves home-made applewine *and* beer, a rare occurrence at Frankfurt applewine taverns.

INFORMATION

- Glauburgstr; Musterschule; Holzhausenstr
- 12
- 30, 36

Martin Moos

Martin Moos

Holzhausen Park's little castle

Well-Heeled Holzhausen

Famous Frankfurt architect and town planner Ernst May had his studio in the moated Holzhausenschlösschen from 1913 until the end of WWI, and designed many of the houses in the surrounding streets including Fürstenbergerstrasse and Kleebergstrasse. Known as the Holzhausen quarters, after the Holzhausen family that held the office of town mayor on around 70 occasions during the 1300s, this is one of the most affluent districts of Frankfurt.

PALMENGARTEN & GRÜNEBURGPARK (1, D5)

Much of the elegant Westend district was left unscathed during the war, and its showcase houses now shelter Frankfurt's patriarchs, matriarchs and a growing number of yuppies, as well as diplomats and consuls.

Founded over 130 years ago, the **Palmengarten**, or botanic garden, is dominated by the gigantic **Palmenhaus**, one of the world's largest greenhouses. The **Tropicarium** houses a mammoth collection of desert plants and rainforest foliage.

If flesh-eating plants and subtropical greenhouses aren't your thing, take a stroll around the 22 hectares of parkland. Here you'll find a boating pond, a miniature railway for the wee ones, as well as artists sketching the many statues and sculptures dotted around the grounds, and an expensive cafe. Sunday morning jazz in summer captures it all. Numerous art and gardening courses are on offer at the Palmengarten, and the **Galerie-Ost** hosts changing art and plant exhibitions.

The Palmengarten is adjoined by the popular **Grüneburgpark**, Frankfurt's 2nd-largest inner city park after Ostpark (p. 40). Joggers, cyclists, walkers and people-watchers come in droves at the first hint of sunshine, and it's convenient for the office brigade to drop in and wind down. Bring a picnic and while away the hours. A walk around the north-eastern end reveals an ornate Greek Orthodox chapel, a sudden surprise in this away-from-it-all park.

At the north of the park, a bridge crosses the motorway at Miquelallee and leads into the **Deutsche Bundesbank** grounds (1, C5). Now demoted to the rank and file beneath the European Central Bank, the bank still casts an impressive shadow across the parklands.

Martin Moos

INFORMATION

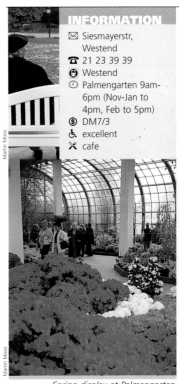

- ✉ Siesmayerstr, Westend
- ☎ 21 23 39 39
- Westend
- Palmengarten 9am-6pm (Nov-Jan to 4pm, Feb to 5pm)
- $ DM7/3
- ♿ excellent
- ✕ cafe

Martin Moos

Spring display at Palmengarten

DON'T MISS

- coffee at the Park Cafe pavilion in Grüneburgpark
- paddle-boating in the Palmengarten

RÖMERBERG & PAULSPLATZ (3, C2)

Welcome to what you think you see. It may not look like it, but the Römerberg square at the centre of Frankfurt's old town is a reconstruction. Bombing raids in March 1944 flattened the historic Römerberg and its surrounds. The restoration began in earnest in the 1980s when the timber-framed houses on the east flank were rebuilt. Check out the **Historisches Museum** (3, D2; p. 36) to the south of the square for before-and-after models.

The Römerberg is usually the first stop on the visitor's trail, and has one of Frankfurt's three tourist offices at the north-west corner. It's also the scene of many open-air festivals including the Weihnachtsmarkt (Christmas market), which runs for 4 weeks before the holiday. During the annual Mainfest in August, the **Fountain of Justice** at the centre of the square doubles as a source for applewine, the local poison that grows on you the more you imbibe.

Transport yourself back in time to when Frankfurt was the coronation capital for the Holy Roman Emperors that ruled this part of the world. From the 16th to 18th centuries, 10 emperors were crowned, with much pomp and ceremony, in the **Kaiserdom** (3, C4), the Cathedral of the Emperors, on Domplatz. The Dommuseum is rich with relics from the 14th century to today relating the dramatic history of the Dom. Unfortunately, the tower and viewing gallery

INFORMATION

- ☎ Paulskirche 21 23 49 09, 21 23 85 26; Kaiserdom 13 37 61 86
- Römer; Hauptwache
- 11
- Paulskirche 10am-5pm; Kaiserdom 9am-noon, 2.30-6pm (Fri & Sun 2.30-6pm only)
- $ free (Dommuseum DM2)
- ⓘ Tourist Information Office, Römerberg 27, ☎ 21 23 87 08, 9.30am-5pm (Sat-Sun to 4pm)
- ♿ good

Martin Moos

Martin Moos

Rententurm, medieval tower of the Historical Museum, Römerberg

DON'T MISS

- Braubachstrasse for its art galleries and curiosity shops
- Steinernes Haus restaurant, Römerberg's first stone building
- prize-winning cake shop Konditorei Hollhorst

are closed for an unspecified period due to renovation.

The **Schirn Kunsthalle** art gallery (3, C3; p. 37) is a misfit among the timber-framed buildings and Roman archaeological remains at the foot of the Dom. But it's one of the city's finest exhibition halls. It was on this site that traders sold their wares in the days of old, sowing the seeds of Frankfurt's trading tradition. The trestle table they used was known as a Schirn, and the name stuck. The Schirn cafe/restaurant is a loud but elegant spot to grab a coffee or meal.

Celebrations on High

Frenchman Philippe Petit walked a tightrope between the Paulskirche and the Dom in July 1994 to mark Frankfurt's 1200th anniversary. The artiste entertained more than a million people watching with bated breath below as he danced his way across.

On the west flank of the square is the stern-looking town hall, called the **Römer**, where 93 local parliamentarians quibble over city policy.

A stone's throw away at Paulsplatz, the **Paulskirche** (3, B1) is a monument to Germany's democratic movement. St Paul's Church was the seat of Germany's first freely elected national assembly in 1848, where the representatives drafted a binding constitution, which became the cornerstone of Germany's law. The plenary chamber where this happened is now only used on special ceremonial occasions. Johannes Grützke's mural is a dramatic depiction of the procession of the people's representatives to the Paulskirche parliament.

The row of pizzerias and gelaterias at the square is a popular spot to people-watch and soak up the sun.

Martin Moos

Fountain of Justice and the Ostzeile half-timbered houses, Römerberg

SACHSENHAUSEN (2, K7)

Much as its inhabitants recoil from being associated with their neighbours across the river, Sachsenhausen offers more than just a passing glimpse of the 'real' Frankfurt, with its boisterous taverns, rustic restaurants and trundling trams. The main attractions of this classic tourist magnet come in two neat packages: Schweizer Strasse and Alt-Sachsenhausen.

INFORMATION

- Lokalbahnhof; Schweizer Platz
- 14, 15, 16
- 30, 36, 46

Martin Moos

Die Frau Rauscher
aus de Klappergaß,
die hot e Beul am Ei.
Ob's vom Rauscher,
ob's vom Alte kimmt,
das klärt die Polizei.

Martin Moos

Frau Rauscher, a monument to applewine

Schweizer Strasse has evolved into an upmarket shopping street lined with boutiques, delicatessens, wine arcades and the odd supermarket. It's also got its fill of trendy bistros, wine bars and local haunts. The airy Cafe Wega is one of the newest additions. **Schweizer Platz** takes centre stage with residential streets emanating in all directions. Saturday afternoon in Haus Wagner is a local ritual. If seats prove hard to come by, try Kanonensteppel or Germania on Textorstrasse, or Fichtekränzi in the Abtsgasse.

Cobblestoned **Alt-Sachsenhausen** (2, J10) is the rough-and-ready part of the neighborhood, as revellers get down to the serious business of boozing and cruising. The streets are decked with outdoor seating in summer and music pumps from every window. It's a popular haunt for off-duty GIs. Check out the Klappergasse for **Frau Rauscher**, the old woman who spits.

Rental prices in downtown Sachsenhausen are affordable. The squeeze experienced in the mid-1990s has passed, as a spate of new construction eased demand all over Frankfurt. Apartments in century-old *Altbau* buildings are much sought after with their high ceilings and wooden floors, while luxury apartments on the hilltop Sachsenhäuser Berg are desirable residences among expats.

DON'T MISS

- flea market on the south river embankment (Sat 9am-2pm)
- *Handkäse mit Musik* washed down with a glass of applewine
- Eiscafe Milano on Schweizer Strasse, for cold ice cream on a hot day

STÄDELSCHES KUNSTINSTITUT & STÄDTISCHE GALERIE (2, K6)

Frankfurt's most prestigious art gallery, the Städel, commands attention when it's lit up like a beacon in the night. The core collection is of German and Dutch Masters of the 17th and 18th centuries. A valuable impressionist and postimpressionist collection includes Renoir's *La fin du déjeuner*. Dissatisfied with his painting *Die Orchestermusiker*, Edgar Degas asked for it to be returned in 1874 so he could rework it. A barely discernible line across the top third of the painting denotes the changes.

This is one of Frankfurt's most 'touchy-feely' exhibition halls, with student groups and budding artists sitting engaged in lectures and sketching lessons in every nook and cranny of the mammoth building. Vernissages (openings) and cultural events are a regular occurrence, as are parties and piano music in Holbein's bistro/restaurant.

The attached Städel school has produced a steady stream of local artists who occupy studio space all over the city and hold regular exhibitions at some of the city's private art galleries. Some even make it into the Museum of Modern Art. It was here that expressionist Max Beckmann taught for almost 20 years before fleeing as the Nazis began wielding their power in 1933.

Paintings by Paul Klee, Frank Marc, Edvard Munch and Pablo Picasso are also prized possessions of the Städel foundation.

Tours in German are available every hour (free on Wednesday). Arrange tours in English in advance.

Martin Moos

INFORMATION

- ✉ Schaumainkai 63, Sachsenhausen
- ☎ 605 09 80
- Ⓤ Schweizer Platz
- 🚌 46
- 🕐 Tues-Sun 10am-5pm (Wed to 8pm)
- $ DM10
- ♿ excellent

Martin Moos

Poster for an exhibition at the Städelsches Kunstinstitut

DON'T MISS

- Tischbein's painting of Goethe in Tuscany, a cheesy icon of Frankfurt
- giant-sized Holbein's bistro, good for observing the arty-farty types

VOLKSPARK NIDDATAL & NIDDA VALLEY (1, B2)

Sporting enthusiasts won't be able to resist a cycle along the Nidda tributary that flows into the Main at Frankfurt-Höchst. But with city express and subway stops dotted all along the Nidda, walkers too can take a quick ride out to a number of destinations or visit one of the excellent open-air swimming pools along this mini-valley.

INFORMATION

- Bad Vilbel; Berkersheim; Hausener Weg; Niddapark; Weisser Stein
- 34

Martin Moos

Martin Moos

Cycling through parkland alongside the Nidda tributary

A suggestion for a lengthy bike ride would be the 2½hr round-trip from Bornheim through Seckbach and Enkheim to **Bad Vilbel** (5, B8), and then west along the Nidda to **Höchst** (5, C6; p. 19). A quick ferry ride across the river (boats stop at 8pm) will take you to a well-marked-out cycle route that stretches east along the south side of the Main through Schwanheim to Sachsenhausen.

Nidda valley residents are blessed with a number of outdoor swimming pools. The **Brentanobad** (1, D1; p. 45) at Rödelheimer Parkweg is Europe's biggest open-air pool, stretching a curved 220m. The **Freibad Eschersheim** (p. 45) at Eschersheim/Heddernheim is also a popular destination.

The Palmengarten is the only other place you'll see foliage like the heathers and mosses growing in the **Volkspark Niddatal**. The park was created in the late 1980s when Frankfurt hosted the *Bundesgartenschau*, or National Garden Show, and its 168 hectares provide enough walking space to keep you going for days. The park is particularly appealing for its apparent unruliness. It's not manicured to perfection and is the biggest of the few true nature reserves around.

DON'T MISS

- a beer at micro-brewery Wäldches, Am Ginnheimer Wäldchen
- Hundertwasser's colourful kindergarten with quirky shapes and turrets
- 'New Frankfurt' housing projects (designed by Ernst May) at Hadrianstrasse, Im Heidenfeld and An der Ringmauer

FRANKFURT ZOO (2, E13)

A camel posse representing Sultan Suleyman II at the coronation of Kaiser Maximilian II in 1562 wasn't the impetus to found the zoological gardens in Frankfurt, but it was the start of the city's affair with exotic animals. The zoo opened in 1858 and moved to its present location at Alfred-Brehm-Platz in 1874.

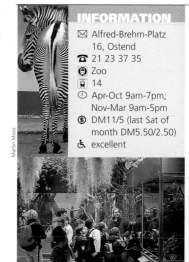

Today it's recognised as one of the most significant zoos in Europe, especially for its nocturnal house and Exotarium. It's situated in the heart of residential Ostend, and neighbours are regularly treated to the howling of wolves and the panting of the baboons.

Timing it right, you can participate in the animals' daily routine. The most exciting events of the day are the tropical storms, at 11.30am and 3.30pm, when the animals in the **Exotarium** are kept in touch with their natural environment with simulated storms. This house in the centre of the grounds is also the main focus of the zoo's activities. The pelicans, seals and monkeys get fed twice daily at 10.30am, and 2.15, 4.10 and 4.30pm, respectively. Penguins dine at 10.45am and 3.45pm daily except Friday. Water turtles feed on Monday and Thursday at 3pm, and the crocodiles on Thursday at 3.15pm. Watch the piranhas' feeding frenzy on Sunday and Wednesday at 11am and 3pm.

It will take a few minutes to adjust your eyes to the 'moonlight' in the **nocturnal house**, but then hundreds of bright eyes will begin staring out at you from the rows of glass cabins.

Martin Moos

INFORMATION

- ✉ Alfred-Brehm-Platz 16, Ostend
- ☎ 21 23 37 35
- U-Bahn: Zoo
- Tram: 14
- Apr-Oct 9am-7pm; Nov-Mar 9am-5pm
- $ DM11/5 (last Sat of month DM5.50/2.50)
- ♿ excellent

Martin Moos

Exploring the Exotarium

Martin Moos

Wrinkled resident rhino

DON'T MISS

- the exotic beer garden Zoo Terrassen, which opens in the evening after the zoo has closed

sights & activities

There's more to Frankfurt than meets the eye. Apart from its excellent collection of museums along the embankment, there is also a huge array of private art galleries. And, despite the city's war damage, there are intact buildings of historical significance and monuments worth a closer look.

About a third of Frankfurt is parkland, so it's easy to find a lush spot away from the bustle and the high-rises. The public transport system runs like clockwork, and you can be outside the city in 20 minutes. Much of Frankfurt is navigable on foot, and the whole region is a haven for cyclists and outdoor enthusiasts.

The previous chapter highlighted some of the most popular districts; others worth exploring include the following.

Fressgasse & Surrounds

Ask for this street by its real name, Grosse Bockenheimer Strasse (2, E6), and you'll be hard put to find someone who can point you in the right direction. Known locally as Fressgasse, or 'Chow Alley', it's a dense collection of sandwich bars, upmarket delis, brasseries, restaurants and fast-food joints. Fur-coated old ladies and poodles are mid-morning sights, but the proprietors really earn their bread and butter with the frenzied midday rush of business suits.

After dark, expat hangouts on Kaiserhofstrasse and wine bars on Kleine Hochstrasse keep the oil lamps burning.

The Fressgasse and the adjoining Goethestrasse have always been a bit hoity-toity, with the bourgeoisie from Kaiserstrasse and the south bank villas promenading their length. Nowadays, just about anyone struts their stuff here – with the obligatory mobile phone. Kaiserstrasse has some fine examples of Belle Epoque architecture.

The Kleine Bockenheimer Strasse, or 'Jazz Alley', is where Frankfurt's jazz scene flowered in the 50s. North, in the Opernplatz, is the Alte Oper (1888), the main classical music venue. During summer, the Fressgasse and Opernplatz set the scene for endless wine and gourmet festivals.

Prima Donna No More

The facade of the Alte Oper was rebuilt, brick by brick, in 1981 after years of heated political debate that had almost sent it to its grave. A new opera house, at Willy-Brandt-Platz, has taken over the diva role, and the Alte Oper is now viewed as a white elephant struggling to regain its former glory. It's used for popular concerts and events, and hosts its own classical concert series.

Martin Moos

Detail of the Old Opera House facade

Hanauer Landstrasse

The city's derelict, formerly industrial east end was transformed in the mid-1990s into a haven for architects, designers, artists, car dealers and small businesses, taking advantage of the ridiculously low rents.

Dormant factories and docklands made ideal studio space, and before long some of Frankfurt's nightlife scene also moved in. You can party all night long on Hanauer Landstrasse (1, F10), the main artery, as there's little passing trade and no interfering neighbours.

Some of the city's leading clubs, gay and straight, draw huge crowds to the district, and many good restaurants are also moving in.

For an impressive example of local architecture, catch a night-time glimpse of the transparent J Walter Thompson building.

Beware: the Hanauer Landstrasse's wide traffic stream and relatively few traffic lights make it treacherous for pedestrians. And always carry a taxi phone number, as public transport stops around midnight.

Resurgence of the River

The Main River is slowly regaining the prominence it held in the 1920s and 30s as a congregation point for Frankfurters. Back then, the area along the north bank close to the main train station (Hauptbahnhof) was known as the Nizza, or Frankfurt's Nice. A roller-skating rink, a boardwalk decked with palm trees and 3 swimming pools provided the city's main public attraction. Nowadays, there's a good chance you'd emerge glowing if you jumped into the river after dark as the water is replete with unmentionable factory by-products from nearby industrial towns.

But it seems the voices that have long derided the authorities for allowing the river banks to become so shabby are finally getting an ear, and a plan to revive the embankment with housing and entertainment has begun. New housing blocks on the old slaughterhouse site at Deutschherrn-ufer will soon be joined by a complex at the Westhafen behind the Hauptbahnhof.

The best way to view the changes to the city and appreciate its growing skyline is to take a boat ride (p. 54) along the river. But don't allow your imagination to run away with you; this is not a cruise around the canals of Amsterdam or Strasbourg.

Martin Moos

River boats on the Main, passing the Historisches Museum and Kaiserdom's spire

LANDMARKS & NOTABLE BUILDINGS

Behrens Gebäude
(5, C6) Welcome to Gotham City. The Behrens building, former executive headquarters of the Hoechst chemical plant, looks like a set for a Fritz Lang film. It's a stunning example of architect Peter Behrens' expressionist style, and definitely worth the short trip out of town to view. They don't make buildings like this any more.
✉ Industrie Park, Höchst ☎ 305 66 66 Ⓢ Höchst ⌚ Mon-Fri 9am-4pm $ free ♿ good

Börse (2, E7)
At the Frankfurt stock exchange, Europe's largest in terms of turnover, visitors can join journalists in the viewing gallery by presenting ID. Sadly, electronic trading has silenced the mayhem of the floor trade, but share fever has gripped the German public. Staff are on hand to answer queries.
✉ Börsenplatz ☎ 21 010 ⓔ www.exchange.de Ⓢ Hauptwache ⌚ Mon-Fri 10.30am-1.30pm $ free ♿ good

Eschenheimer Turm
(2, D7) This is the only remaining portal of an original 60 dotted along the old city walls. In its most recent history, the late-Gothic gateway (1428) has housed numerous bistros, hoping to make the Tor a nightlife attraction. The latest appears to have succeeded.
✉ Grosse Eschenheimer Str Ⓢ Eschenheimer Tor

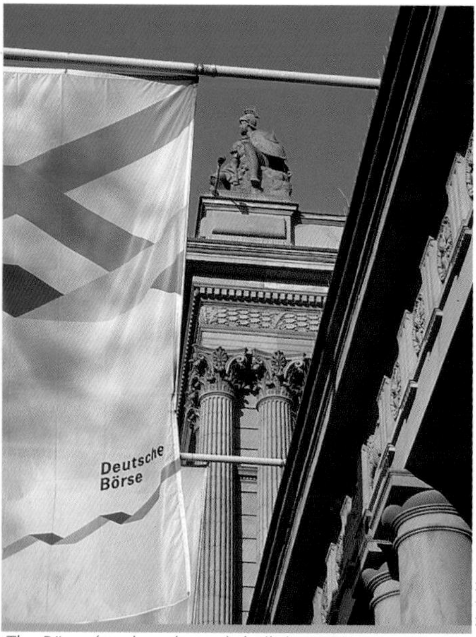

Martin Moos

The Börse (stock exchange), built in 1874

Goetheturm (1, J10)
Maybe a walk in the Stadtwald in the footsteps of Frankfurt's literary son, Goethe, will have you waxing lyrical about the view from the top of this 43m tower dedicated to him. It's claimed to be the highest wooden tower in Germany. Below are playground facilities, and the Goethrüh beer garden is a popular watering hole for cyclists and ramblers. There's a barbecue area on the way eastward to the forest near Buchrainweg.
✉ Am Goetheturm, Sachsenhausen 🚌 30, 36, Babenhäuser Landstr ⌚ open May-Sept $ free ♿ good

Grossmarkthalle
(2, G13) Architecture fans will be interested in the giant Grossmarkthalle fruit and vegetable wholesale market (built 1928). Now a protected building, it's the finest example of town planner and visionary Ernst May's *Neue Frankfurt* concept. In its darkest moment it was used as an assembly point to transport Jews out of the city to concentration camps. Today the survival of this rather dilapidated building is the subject of controversy among local politicians.
✉ Sonnemannstr, Ostend ☎ 21 23 36 93 Ⓢ Ostbahnhof ⌚ Mon-Fri 4-11am ♿ good

Hammering Man (4, D5) A symbol of labour, this Jonathan Borovsky sculpture was erected in 1991 to mark the completion of the Messeturm. Standing 21.5m tall, he has become a city landmark and a welcoming figure at the western motorway entry point to the city.
✉ **Friedrich-Ebert-Anlage, Westend**
🚊 **16, 19, Messe**

Hauptwache (2, F7) This fine example of baroque architecture is in remarkably good shape considering it was dismantled in the 1980s to make way for subway construction and then rebuilt. Dating from 1730, and originally the town's main watch or sentry point, it once served as a prison, but has been a cafe since 1904.
✉ **An der Hauptwache**
Ⓤ **Hauptwache**

IG Farbenhaus/ Poelzig-Bau (2, A4) This bombastic piece of architecture (1931) by expressionist Hans Poelzig was once the headquarters of the IG Farben chemical conglomerate which made Zyklon B, the gas used in Nazi concentration camps. Later this 7-storey monstrosity was known as Europe's 'Pentagon', when it was US General Eisenhower's military headquarters.
✉ **Fürstenbergerstr/ Grüneburgplatz, Westend**
Ⓤ **Grüneburgweg**

Karmeliterkloster & Museum für Vor- und Frügeschichte (2, G7) A tranquil spot in the inner city, this late-Gothic monastery is one of Frankfurt's most treasured cultural assets. Once used as a barracks, it was originally home to the Carmelite order of monks. The Renaissance frescoes in the refectory and cloister comprise one of Central Europe's most important collections. The complex now houses the Museum of Pre- and Early History, and the Institut für Stadtgeschichte, a photo archive of the city.
✉ **Münzgasse 9 (Museum: Karmelitergasse 1)** ☎ **21 23 84 25 (Museum: 21 23 58 96)**
Ⓤ **Willy-Brandt-Platz**
🕘 **8.30am-5pm (Sat-**

Charlotte Hindle

The Messe's Hammering Man

Martin Moos

The Hauptwache, at the very heart of the city

Reach for the Sky

Frankfurt's rapidly expanding skyline includes the following high-flyers:

Europa-Turm	331m	Wilhelm-Epstein-Str
Commerzbank	298m	Kaiserplatz
Messeturm	256m	Friedrich-Ebert-Anlage
DG Bank	208m	Mainzer Landstr 58
Main Tower Helaba	200m	Neue Mainzer Str
Deutsche Bank	155m	Taunusanlage 12
European Central Bank	148m	Kaiserstr 29
Henninger Turm	120m	Hainer Weg
Japan Center	114m	Taunustor/Neue Mainzer Str
Dom	95m	Domstr

Martin Moos

Reflections of night lights on the Main River

Sun from 10am) ⓢ free ♿ good

Kleinmarkthalle

(3, A3) Frankfurt's first fresh food market started up here after the war. Now the Kleinmarkthalle is a bustling food hall with over 100 stands selling fruit and vegetables, exotic fruits and spices, fresh meats, cured sausage and fish. Restaurants and consumers pay handsomely for the privilege to shop here.
✉ Zeigelgasse/An der Kleinmarkthalle
Ⓤ Hauptwache
⏲ Mon-Fri 7.30am-6pm, Sat 7.30am-3pm
♿ good

Liebfrauenkirche

(3, A2) People of all religions are drawn to this inner-city sanctuary, where a secluded churchyard exudes a permanent warmth from the thousands of burning candles lit by passers-by every day. The Capuchin monks and nuns feed Frankfurt's homeless.
✉ Liebfrauenstr
Ⓤ Hauptwache
⏲ Mon-Fri 6.30am-6pm ♿ good

Market Art

Check out the giant mural entitled *Frankfurt Panorama* (1997) hanging inside the Liebfrauenberg entrance to the Kleinmarkthalle. An American professor of architecture, Douglas Cooper, produced this depiction of Frankfurt based on interviews with thousands of Frankfurters.

Westend Synagogue

(2, B3) This is the only Frankfurt synagogue to survive the *Reichskristallnacht* in November 1938, but it did suffer damage from torching and the 1944 bombing raids. The synagogue was renovated and re-inaugurated in 1950.
✉ Freiherr-vom-Stein-Str/Altkönigstr, Westend Ⓤ Westend

MUSEUMS

Information overload maybe but it's possible to get around Frankfurt's museums in a weekend as most of them are handily located around the river banks. The **Museum Embankment** was conceived in the 1980s in an egalitarian gesture of 'culture for all'. The city spent buckets restoring the aristocratic mansions on the south bank, and added exhibition space like the Schirn's long hall and rotunda – or 'Murder at the Cathedral' as some local wits call it – and the angular Museum of Modern Art. Now some 16 museums, dominated by the Städel Art Institute (p. 27), are located in the immediate vicinity.

Avoid Sunday afternoon visits unless you fancy battling your way through the throngs. Wednesday's a better bet, when most museums are free and stay open longer.

Children, students, pensioners and the unemployed usually pay half-price. Do avail yourself of the 'Museumsufer Ticket', a DM15 (students DM7.50) 2-day pass to all the museums on the embankment and any touring exhibitions on display (available at most museums). Regrettably, many exhibitions are only explained in German. Tours in English can be arranged in advance, but could take a few days to organise and are expensive.

Don't miss the annual Museumsuferfest, festival of the museums, in mid-August.

Deutsches Architekturmuseum (2, J6) The Architecture Museum has a broad appeal with its hands-on approach and topical exhibitions. Renowned architect Oswald Mathias Ungers transformed this patrician villa in 1984 with his controversial 'house within a house' concept. Frankfurt's town planning policy is frequent fodder for debate. Claustrophobes be warned, though.
✉ Schaumainkai 43, Sachsenhausen ☎ 21 23 88 44 Ⓤ Willy-Brandt-Platz; Schweizer Platz 🚍 46 ⏲ Tues-Sun 10am-5pm (Wed to 8pm) $ DM8 ♿ good

Deutsches Filmmuseum (2, J7) Here you might be rewarded with a Greta Garbo photographic retrospective or a director's tribute. Sadly, it must be said that the exhibitions often lack substance. These are usually combined with a film season, often in English, in the cinema downstairs (see p. 98). Upstairs is a collection of film memorabilia and equipment.
✉ Schaumainkai 41, Sachsenhausen ☎ 21 23 33 69 Ⓤ Willy-Brandt-Platz; Schweizer Platz 🚍 46 ⏲ Tues-Sun 10am-5pm (Wed to 8pm, Sat 2-8pm) $ DM5 ♿ good ✕ cafe

Geld Museum der Deutschen Bundesbank (1, C5) Frankfurt was the birthplace of 2 major currencies in the last century, so it is fitting that the Deutsche Bundesbank, Germany's central bank, should house the Money Museum, on the history of money, and foreign exchange and monetary policy. It's one of the

Martin Moos

The Filmmuseum houses the largest collection of German film available.

few also explained in English.
✉ **Wilhelm-Epppstein-Str 14, Dornbusch ☎ 95 66 30 73 ⓔ www.bundesbank.de Ⓜ Dornbusch; Miquel-/Adickesallee 🚌 34 ⏲ 10am-7pm (Wed 1-9pm) $ free ♿ good**

Historisches Museum
(3, D2) Tracing Frankfurt's history from the days of Charlemagne, the History Museum has a strong emphasis on the Roman period and late-medieval Frankfurt. Visit the apple-wine museum, or enjoy a Sunday jazz brunch held occasionally in summer in the garden yard.
✉ **Saalgasse 19 ☎ 21 23 55 99 Ⓜ Römer 🚋 11 ⏲ Tues-Sun 10am-5pm (Wed to 8pm) $ DM8 ♿ good**

Höchster Porzellan im Dalberger Haus
(5, C6) You get the feeling that if you sneezed, all the delicate pieces of porcelain would shatter at this museum devoted to the exquisite Höchst Porcelain. There are video presentations in German, English and Japanese.
✉ **Bolongarostr 186, Höchst ☎ 300 90 20 Ⓜ Höchst ⏲ Mon-Thurs 9am-1pm, 2-4.30pm, Fri 9am-2pm $ free; group tours DM80 ♿ excellent**

Martin Moos

Make contact at the Museum für Kommunikation

The Jewish Museum portrays the history of Frankfurt's Jews

Jüdisches Museum
(2, H6) This former home of the Rothschild banking family today houses the extensive Jewish Museum detailing Frankfurt's role in the Holocaust and the history and culture of the city's Jewish community. A wooden model shows the now-disappeared Jewish ghetto of the Middle Ages.
✉ **Untermainkai 14-15 ☎ 21 23 50 00 Ⓜ Willy-Brandt-Platz ⏲ Tues-Sun 10am-5pm (Wed to 8pm) $ DM5 ♿ excellent (entrance at Hofstr 9)**

Museum für Kommunikation
(2, K6) Children love this museum with its kiddies' workshop and hands-on exhibits. Adults will also be fascinated by exhibits such as Cold War espionage equipment. Find out about the 583m tunnel the CIA and MI6 dug under the Schönfelder Chaussee in East Berlin, or how to make invisible ink.

✉ **Schaumainkai 53, Sachsenhausen** ☎ **606 00** Ⓤ **Schweizer Platz** 🚌 **46** ⏲ **Tues-Fri 9am-5pm, Sat-Sun 11am-7pm** $ **free** ♿ **good**

Museum für Kunsthandwerk **(2, J8)** The Museum of Applied Arts is one of the most eye-catching museums in Frankfurt, housed in this 1804 villa redesigned by New Yorker Richard Meier in 1985. Its changing exhibitions focusing on graphics, product design and modern appliances complement the permanent display of cultural objects from all over the world.
✉ **Schaumainkai 17, Sachsenhausen** ☎ **21 23 40 37** Ⓤ **Schweizer Platz** 🚌 **46** ⏲ **Tues-Sun 10am-5pm (Wed to 8pm)** $ **DM8** ♿ **good**

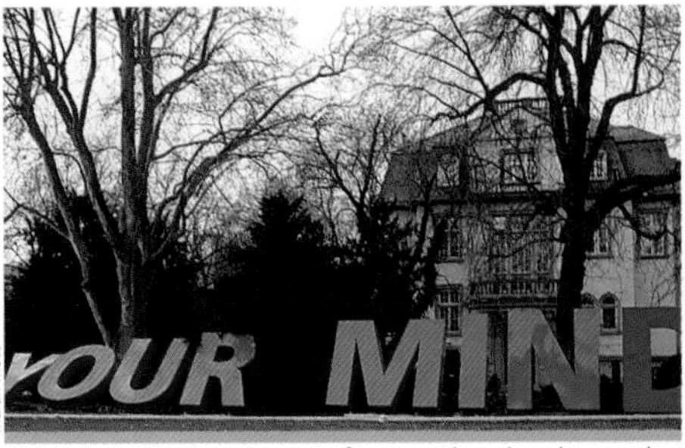

Martin Moos

Display in the Museum für Kunsthandwerk's garden (Ethnological Museum in the background)

Museum Judengasse **(3, B5)** The Judengasse was a ghetto to which Frankfurt's Jews were banished in the Middle Ages (p. 6). The cellars and ritual baths of 3 houses from this alley are now preserved in a small museum. There's also an extensive archive remembering Frankfurt's Holocaust victims, and a cemetery behind.
✉ **Kurt-Schumacher-Str 10** ☎ **297 74 19** Ⓤ **Konstablerwache** 🚋 **11** 🚌 **36** ⏲ **Tues-Sun 10am-5pm (Wed to 8pm)** $ **DM3 (free Sat), group tours in English DM80** ♿ **excellent**

GALLERIES

Frankfurt has many public galleries, and almost 50 private art galleries mostly concentrated around the Dom and Braubachstrasse, Sachsenhausen and Hanauer Landstrasse. The quarterly magazine *Art Kaleidoscope*, available at most newsagents for DM5, is in both German and English and lists current exhibitions.

PUBLIC GALLERIES

Frankfurter Kunstverein (3, C3) This association of Frankfurt artists is still going strong almost 200 years after its founding. The emphasis is on multimedia and provocative art, with changing exhibitions by renowned contemporary artists. Cultural identity is a recurring theme.
✉ **Steinernes Haus am Römerberg, Markt 44** ☎ **28 53 39** Ⓤ **Römer** 🚋 **11** ⏲ **Tues-Sun 11am-8pm** $ **DM8** ♿ **good**

Schirn Kunsthalle **(3, C3)** Without a permanent collection, the Schirn Art Gallery has a freedom of expression that other Frankfurt art institutions don't have. The 'bowling alley' and rotunda exhibition halls compete for attention with touring displays, from ancient Italian cultures to modern Japanese artists.
✉ **Römerberg** ☎ **299 88 20** Ⓤ **Römer** 🚋 **11** ⏲ **Wed-Sat 11am-10pm, Tues & Sun 11am-7pm** $ **DM15** ♿ **excellent**

Städtische Galerie Liebieghaus Museum Alter Plastik (2, K5) This gallery is dedicated to ancient and pre-modern sculpture linking Egyptian, Greek and Roman works with Renaissance and medieval exponents. A generous number of sculptures

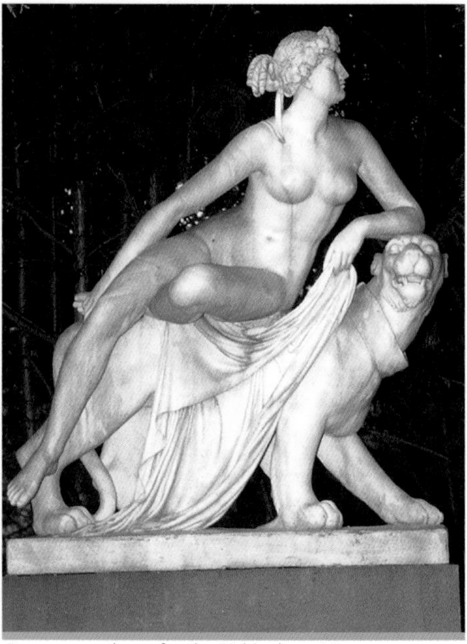

Dress up or down for the Liebieghaus Museum

are planted in the gardens, making a walk through the grounds an absolute must.
✉ **Schaumainkai 71, Sachsenhausen ☎ 21 23 86 12 Ⓤ Schweizer Platz 🚌 46 ⏲ Tues-Sun 10am-5pm (Wed to 8pm) $ DM5 ♿ good ✕ Cafe im Liebieghaus**

PRIVATE GALLERIES

Amerika Haus (2, C4)
This cultural institute was founded to foster American-German ties in the postwar period. Exhibitions range from painting to photography, and there are concerts, recitals and readings.
✉ **Staufenstr 1, Westend**
☎ 971 44 80
@ www.usembassy.de
Ⓤ Alte Oper ⏲ Mon-Fri 10am-7pm $ free
♿ good

Bärbel Grässlin
(2, D8) The focus here is on painting and sculpture by German artists of the 1980s. The gallery doesn't seem to suffer from its isolated location.
✉ **Bleichstr 48 ☎ 28 09 61 Ⓤ Eschenheimer Tor 🚌 36 ⏲ Tues-Fri 10am-6pm, Sat 10am-2pm $ free**
♿ good

Bernauer Berg
(2, K9) German post-expressionists from 1910 through the Dritte Reich period are on show here.
✉ **Textorstr 58, Sachsenhausen**
☎ 62 87 44
Ⓤ Südbahnhof 🚊 14
⏲ Tues-Fri 2-6.30pm (Thurs to 8pm), Sat 12-2pm $ free

Bernd Slutzky (1, G4)
This shows 20th-century graphic and photographic art and works by Städel graduates.
✉ **Frankenallee 74, Gallusviertel ☎ 72 39 40 Ⓤ Galluswarte**
⏲ Mon-Fri 11am-6pm, Sat 11am-4pm $ free

Exler Aussereuropäische Kunst (3, C5)
Exhibits African and Latin American art and artefacts.
✉ **Fahrgasse 6**
☎ 28 38 18 @ www.artnet.com/exler.html
Ⓤ Römer 🚊 11
⏲ Tues-Fri 2-6pm, Sat 11am-4pm $ free

Fotografie Forum International (3, C4)
From fashion to art to photojournalism, this gallery-museum is the only exhibition space in Frankfurt entirely devoted to photography. It also hosts the award-winning World Press Photo collection every 2 years (December or January).
✉ **Weckmarkt 17**
☎ 29 17 26 Ⓤ Römer 🚊 11 ⏲ Tues-Fri 11am-6pm (Wed to 8pm), Sat-Sun 11am-5pm $ DM6 ♿ good

Frankfurter Kunstkabinett Hanna Bekker vom Rath
(3, B2) German expressionist art is the main focus at this gallery, one of the longest running in the city. It's been selling its exhibits for over 50 years.
✉ **Braubachstr 14-16**
☎ 28 10 85 @ www.artnet.com/hbekkervo

mrath.html Römer 11 Tues-Fri 11am-6pm, Sat 11am-4pm $ free

Frankfurter Westend Galerie (2, E1) Italy comes to the fore at this Westend gallery, one of the frontrunners in the private art scene in Frankfurt. **Arndtstr 12, Westend ☎ 74 67 52 Westend 33 Tues-Fri 10am-1pm, 3-7pm, Sat 11am-1pm $ free**

Galerie BBK (1, F10) The artists who make these studios their everyday workspace founded this miniature colony in recent years. They're open to the public for a few hours every week, and regular exhibition openings are held also. **Hanauer Landstr 139, Ostend ☎ 49 52 90 Ostbahnhof 11 Tues 11am-8pm, Fri-Sun 4-8pm $ free**

Holzhausenschlösschen (1, D7) The residents of the noble Holzhausen quarter are proud of their moated castle, completed in 1729. The castle hosts exhibitions, often with local themes, organised by a local citizens' initiative. **Justinianstr 5, Nordend ☎ 55 77 91 Holzhausenstrasse 36, Hynspergstrasse Thurs-Sun 11am-5pm (Wed 2-8pm) $ free**

Japan Art (3, B3) The name speaks for itself; this gallery specialises in modern art from the Orient. **Braubachstr 9 ☎ 28 28 39 Römer 11 Tues-Fri 12-7pm, Sat 10am-2pm $ free**

LA Galerie (3, B3) It's got nothing to do with Los Angeles; the name stands for the owner, Lothar Albrecht, who specialises in experimental photography. **Domstr 6 ☎ 28 86 87 Römer 11 Tues-Fri 12-7pm, Sat 11am-4pm $ free**

Niebbiensches Gartenhaus (2, D6) A local artists' initiative organises changing exhibitions, musical recitals and readings in this beautiful garden lodge, built in classical style around 1820, located behind the Hilton Hotel. Sunday matinees begin at 11am. Exhibits are also for sale. **Bockenheimer Anlage ☎ 23 57 34 Eschenheimer Tor Tues-Sun 11am-5pm $ free good**

PARKS, GARDENS & HIDEAWAYS

Bethmann Park (2, C10) Old men play *boules*, budding Kasparovs battle it out on the giant chess board, and young lovers laze around the beautifully tended flower beds in this tiny park, one of Frankfurt's best-kept secrets. The Chinese Garden of Heavenly Peace is in memory of the victims of the Tiananmen Square massacre. **Friedberger Anlage, Bornheim/Nordend Merianplatz 30 7.30am-dusk**

Brentanopark/ Solmspark (1, D-E1) Two adjoining garden parks on an island on the Nidda offer a double treat. The 3.5-hectare Brentanopark has a classical touch with the Gartenhaus, which attracted Goethe on his visits to the Brentano family. Solmspark is crowded with valuable trees. See p. 45 for the Brentanobad outdoor swimming pool. **Auf der Insel, Rödelheim Hausener Weg; Rödelheim 34**

Licht- und Luftbad Niederrad (1, H3) Locals have been coming to this idyllic island hideaway on the Main for almost 100 years. These

Martin Moos

Entrance to the peaceful Chinese Garden at Bethmann Park

'Did you remember to bring the frisbee?'

days, bathing is prohibited, but that needn't stop you from lying back and basking in the sun. A cafe serves a limited range of food. Children will enjoy the sheep and donkeys that trim the grass.
✉ Niederräder Ufer 10, Niederrad ☎ 670 85 56 🚋 15, 19, 21, Heinrich-Hoffmann-Str/ Blutspendedienst ⌚ 10am-dusk (restricted in winter) $ free ♿ good

Ostpark (1, E11)
Join the hordes that head for Frankfurt's largest park to play soccer, softball, frisbee or any other sport imaginable. There's always a race to grab the few barbecue facilities available, so many people bring their own grills. A small kiosk sells cold drinks.
✉ Ostparkstr, Ostend Ⓤ Parlamentsplatz; Eissporthalle

Rosisten Anlage 1 (1, K6) Picture this: at the edge of a club of garden allotments, each replete with roses, is a garden restaurant serving regional French cuisine. Not even the sound of planes preparing to land at Frankfurt Airport nearby disturbs this peaceful setting. Take a discreet stroll around the gardens, where the only rule is the owners must grow roses.
✉ Ziegelhüttenweg 221, Sachsenhausen ☎ 63 19 87 00 Ⓤ Frankfurt-Louisa 🚌 35 ⌚ Tues-Sun 11am-midnight ♿ good

Stadtwald (1, K10)
Running short of a penny, Emperor Karl IV was forced to mortgage part of the outlying forests to Frankfurt city in 1372. Of course, Karl never got his bit of woods back, and the 5000-hectare Stadtwald is Germany's largest municipal forest today. Frankfurters celebrate a unique public holiday called *Wäldchestag*, the Tuesday after Whitsun (usually late May/early June). Businesses and shops close at noon, and Frankfurters head to the forest at the Oberforsthaus near the Waldstadion, to enjoy an afternoon of carousels, sausage and beer.
Ⓤ Frankfurt-Louisa 🚋 14, Oberschweinstiege

QUIRKY FRANKFURT

Applewine Express
A jaunt on this extremely noticeable tram is probably the kitschest thing you could do in Frankfurt, but omitting it would leave a serious gap in your education. The 1hr ride on the *Ebbelwei Express* is an honest offering of Frankfurt's best and worst. Fare includes a bottle of applewine, apple juice or water, and a bag of pretzels. The route goes from Bornheim Mitte via the zoo through the city centre, Bahnhofsviertel and Sachsenhausen, then back again.
☎ 21 32 24 25, 21 22 24 25 ⌚ Fri-Sun & holidays every 40mins 1.30-5.30pm (limited timetable Nov-Mar) $ DM6

Bistro Rosa (1, E6)
Ever eaten *loup de mer* while being stared at by 20 pigs? This classic French bistro may be Frankfurt's smallest restaurant, but the quirky pig motif around the walls also makes it the most original. The name and motif refer to the expensive pink truffle (over DM1000/kg, it's rumoured) served occasionally.
✉ Grüneburgweg 25, Westend ☎ 72 13 80 Ⓤ Grüneburgweg ⌚ Tues-Sat 6pm-midnight

Frankfurt Dippemarkt (3, A4) You could almost mistake the old lady who runs this shop full of wacky beer krugs for one of the items on sale. Some of the pitchers stand over 1m tall. This is a treasure trove of traditional pottery, and a definite port of call if you need a quirky gift.
⊠ **Berliner Str (cnr of Fahrgasse)** ☎ **28 25 59** Ⓤ **Römer; Hauptwache** ⏱ **Mon-Fri 10am-6.30pm, Sat 10am-2pm**

Martin Moos

The Dippemarkt will help you hold your beer

Friedberger Warte (1, B8) Visitors have to negotiate speeding traffic to get to this garden restaurant at the Friedberger Warte, a late-Gothic watchtower in the north-west of the city: it's in the middle of a traffic island! Seating 200, it serves good local fare and, as always, the redoubtable applewine.
⊠ **Friedberger Landstr 360, Nordend** ☎ **59 24 65** 🚌 **30, 34, 69, Friedberger Warte** ⏱ **Tues-Sat 4pm-midnight, Sun & holidays noon-midnight** ♿ **good**

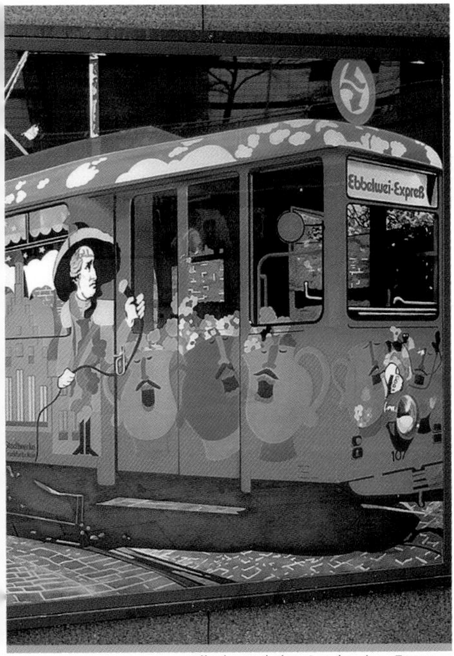

All aboard the Applewine Express

Gute Stute (1, F4) A life-size stuffed horse greets guests at the door of this gem of a pub hidden away in the Gallusviertel. But that's not all that's quirky: swinging chairs hang from the ceiling at the bar. Upstairs is a venue for irregular parties on the independent scene.
⊠ **Kölner Str 42, Gallusviertel** ☎ **730 68 14** Ⓤ **Galluswarte** ⏱ **1pm-1am**

Jazzhouse (2, E6) This tiny pub on Frankfurt's 'Jazz Alley' reeks of nostalgia for the swinging 50s and 60s when American GIs nurtured a talented jazz scene. Haul your drinks up from the bar in a basket via a pulley, but mind the heads of the folks below.
⊠ **Kleine Bockenheimerstr 12** ☎ **28 71 94** Ⓤ **Hauptwache; Alte Oper** ⏱ **Mon-Thurs 5pm-1am, Fri-Sat 5pm-2am**

Käs Kabarett Änderungsschneiderei (2, B7)
Bavarians parodying Frankfurters, Englishmen parodying themselves, Turkish stand-up comedians proving they're really Frankfurters and not 'foreigners', and Frankfurters baring their souls to the world: it can only go downhill from here at this unique stand-up comedy club. Acts are mostly in German.
✉ **Finkenhofstr 17, Nordend** ☎ **55 07 36** Ⓤ **Grüneburgweg** ⌚ **Wed-Sun 6pm-midnight** $ **DM25**

Live from the Südbahnhof (1, H7)
If you thought Germans were a sedate bunch, you won't believe their antics in this music hall at the Südbahnhof train station. In the German tradition of Sunday *Frühschopp'n*, or Sunday morning drinking, guests are entertained by ageing rock bands, who dance on the tables in an atmosphere that brings the house down (Sunday 11am-4pm).
✉ **Diesterwegplatz, Sachsenhausen** ☎ **62 32 01** Ⓤ **Südbahnhof** $ **DM20** ♿ **good**

Brezelmann

A jolly feature of Frankfurt nightlife is the appearance in various pubs and watering holes of the *Brezelmann*, armed with a giant bread basket filled with the last pretzels and cheese rolls of the day, and a bell. These bakers are true Frankfurt characters and receive a hero's welcome in every pub they enter.

Möbel- und Antiquitätenmarkt (2, C14) Underneath the dust and the mites, you might just find a real treasure at this jumble sale-cum-antique market.
✉ **Wittelsbacher Allee 29, Ostend** ☎ **43 56 74, 43 57 55** Ⓤ **Zoo** 🚊 **14** ⌚ **Mon-Fri 8.15am-5.45pm, Sat 8.15am-3.45pm**

Zum Gauss (2, B11)
This is one of a dying breed of 'honest working class' local pubs. Small touches like the northern German Jever pils on tap, and old French and German film posters indicate its worldliness. A small kitchen serves a remarkably good selection of dishes such as crepes with spinach and gorgonzola sauce. This is a real gem.
✉ **Gaussstr 4, Nordend** ☎ **49 89 67** Ⓤ **Merianplatz** ⌚ **Mon-Thurs 6pm-1am, Fri-Sat 6pm-2am**

FRANKFURT FOR CHILDREN

Going by the number of playgrounds in parks and on river banks alone, Frankfurt is a child's paradise. Sandpits and slides are a common feature on the landscape. The subway system and municipal facilities are well served with ramps and escalators, making it easy to get around with pushchairs. See p. 45 for outdoor swimming pools and the Schultheis-Weiher lake. The Senckenberg natural history museum (p. 21) and the Museum für Kommunikation (p. 36) are also kids' favourites.

Explora (1, D7)
What started out as a private collection of puzzles and strange objects is now a museum on the wonders of science, optical illusion and sound, run by the eccentric Gerhard Stief. It's housed in an old bunker once used as a headquarters to prepare the city's final defence in WWII.
✉ **Glauburgplatz, Nordend** ☎ **78 88 88** Ⓤ **Glauburgstr** 🚌 **30** ⌚ **Tues-Sun 11am-6pm** $ **DM11 (DM7/9 children up to/over 12)**

Frankfurter Feldbahnmuseum (1, F1) A love of old field-trains brought this unique transport museum into being. The volunteer club of train enthusiasts collected the 14 steam engines, 12 diesel engines and 100 cars, and laid down the 3km of track. See the brochure in Frankfurter Forum at Römerberg for exact dates of operation.

✉ Am Römerhof 15a, Rebstock ☎ 70 92 92 🚌 30, 34, Römerhof ⏲ 1st Sun of month 2-5pm, closed July/Aug $ DM6/3 ♿ good

Heinrich Hoffmann Museum (3, C3)
Child psychologist Heinrich Hoffmann in 1844 created the 'Slovenly Peter' character now known world-wide as the child who wouldn't cut his hair or fingernails. This tiny museum beneath the Schirn Art Gallery displays the many versions and translations of Hoffmann's books. Costumes are available for children to dress up as the unruly Peter.
✉ Schubertstr 20 ☎ 74 79 69 Ⓤ Römer ⏲ Tues-Sun 10am-5pm $ DM2/1

Historic Steam Train (2, H8) This train runs in the summer months between Ost- and Westhafen, but at irregular times. Climb on at the north end of the Eiserner Steg bridge.
☎ 43 60 93 Ⓤ Römer

Opel Live (5, D5)
This entertainment centre conceived by General Motors subsidiary Adam Opel AG offers a novel look at the world of cars. The interactive multimedia show includes a trip to Opel's new state-of-the-art production facility, simulated rides and a chance to view a crash test.
✉ Friedrich-Lutzmann-Ring 2, Rüsselsheim (25km out of town) ☎ 06142-76 56 00 Ⓢ S8 to Rüsselsheim, then bus 12 ⏲ Apr-Oct: Mon-Fri

Martin Moos

One of Explora's curious exhibits

9am-5pm, Sat-Sun 10am-7pm; Nov-Mar: Wed-Sun only $ DM19/15 ♿ good

Opernspiele (2, E5)/ **Mainspiele** (2, J7)
A group of volunteers provide the inflatable castles, slides, climbing frames and other children's amusements, and organise these summer games at the Opernplatz and the Main River embankment for 6 weeks during the Hesse school holiday (usually in July/August).
✉ Taunusanlage/ Opernplatz; Main River embankment ☎ 299 88 83 33 Ⓤ Alte Oper; Römer

⏲ 11am-dusk $ free ♿ good

Waldspielpark (Scheerwald) (1, J10)
This complex in the forest above Sachsenhausen is the mother of all playgrounds. Walk east along the forest path in front of the Goetheturm (p. 32) for about 600m and hear your children squeal with delight at the collection of slides, mini-carousels, climbing frames and obstacle courses that awaits them.
✉ Am Goetheturm, Sachsenhausen 🚌 30, 36, Sachsenhäuser Warte ♿ good

KEEPING FIT

Golf

There are only 2 golf courses in Frankfurt, but many more in outlying towns such as Bad Homburg (Germany's oldest golf club), Neu-Isenburg, Hanau and Wiesbaden.

Golf in Germany is still the domain of the elite, and membership fees are astronomical (if you manage to get in; membership is often only through recommendation). But green fees for guest players with a handicap and a valid club membership from a recognised club are relatively affordable, starting around DM80. For more information, call Frankfurter Golf-Club e.V. (☎ 666 23 18).

Gyms

There's no shortage of sports studios and muscle shops in Frankfurt. Going to the gym is as much a part of social life as going to the pub, and you'll probably meet the same people in both places. It's possible to go to fitness studios on a daily basis but this will be proportionally more expensive than long-term membership fees. Studios are usually equipped with sauna and steam room facilities, but be aware: nudity rules!

The Web site www.branchen-kompass.de/db.exe?F has a list of fitness studios in Frankfurt – click on Fitness und Sportschulen.

Swimming

Frankfurt may be hundreds of miles from the next nearest sandy ocean beach, but outdoor swimming is still a big leisure activity. The facilities don't usually stop at a swimming pool and changing rooms. Most have enormous grassy parks for sunbathing, and some also offer table tennis and beach volleyball. Alongside the regular swimming pool, there are also usually diving pools, children's pools, slides and fun pools. Outside the city there are many man-made lakes designed to look the part with beaches and boats.

In-line Skating

Roller-blading or in-line skating has taken Frankfurt by storm, and is now an officially recognised form of transport. Go down to the Main river banks any night from May to October, and you will see enthusiasts out practising their skills. Street signs indicate the hours skaters can use the roads.

What began as a weekly gathering of a few skating freaks some years ago has become a Frankfurt institution as, every Tuesday night, thousands of skaters roll through the streets with a police escort between 8.30 and 11pm. Skaters gather 1hr beforehand as flyers with the route are handed out. Departure point is Frankensteinerplatz, Sachsenhausen. It's a great way to meet people if you can skate. Beginners are advised that the pace is competitive – get your skills up to scratch first.

Brentanobad (1, D1) At 220m, this open-air pool is Europe's largest outdoor pool, and is beautifully situated on the Nidda. Beware: it's probably the most popular of all the city's open-air pools and is overrun with visitors especially on hot days. It's also the scene of a summer open-air cinema series that runs between June and September.
✉ **Rödelheimer Parkweg, Rödelheim**
☎ **21 23 90 20**
Am Fischstein
🕘 **May-Aug 7am-8pm**
$ **DM5/2.50**

Fitness Company (2, F6) Runs 6 fitness studios including 2 ladies' health clubs and The Business Club, which attracts expats and members of the business community with corporate membership rates. Also runs a racquet club in Eckenheim.
✉ **Kaiserstr 5a**
☎ **96 37 32 00**
Hauptwache; Willy-Brandt-Platz
🕘 **Mon-Thurs 8am-11pm, Fri 8am-10pm, Sat-Sun 10am-7pm**
♿ **yes**

Between 9 and 5 only, if you're game

Freibad Eschersheim Its curved shape and 156m length make it one of the most unusual swimming pools around. Like many outdoor pools, this one's not heated.
✉ **Im Uhrig, Eschersheim/Heddernheim**
☎ **21 23 21 53**
Heddernheim; Eschersheim; Weisser Stein
🕘 **May-Aug 10am-8pm**
$ **DM5/2.50**

Freibad Hausen (1, C1) This open-air swimming arena has 3 heated swimming pools as well as a children's playground and massive park grounds for sunbathing and playing frisbee.
✉ **Ludwig-Landemann-Str 341, Hausen**
☎ **21 23 41 05** **Am Fischstein** 🕘 **Apr-Sept 7am-7pm (to 8pm May-Aug)** $ **DM5/2.50**

Golf Waldstadion Small-scale golf course (9 or 12 holes), with driving range, putting green, all-weather greens. No club membership needed.
✉ **Mörfelder Landstr 362, Niederrad** ☎ **67 80 42 22** **19, Stadion** **61** 🕘 **9am-dusk**
$ **green fees: DM30**

Paragon Golf Akademie (1, J4) A new concept aiming to zap elitism in golf, the inner area of the horse racing course has been converted to an 18-hole golf links for use on non-racing days. There's a driving range and equipment rental.
✉ **Schwarzwaldstr 127, Niederrad**
☎ **96 74 13 53** **19** **61, Rennbahnstr**
🕘 **usually 9am-dusk**
$ **green fees: 9 holes Mon-Fri DM40, Sat-Sun DM45; 18 holes Mon-Fri DM80, Sat-Sun DM90; driving range Mon-Fri DM15, Sat-Sun DM20**

Schultheis-Weiher (1, C15) Most people travel here by bike, the direct route to this recultivated nature reserve and lake at Bürgel, Offenbach. From the tram stop in Fechenheim, it's a 10-minute walk, or a good 20-minute walk from the Mainkur S-Bahn stop. But definitely go, if only to see how Frankfurters adapt to living so far inland. Swimming is permitted in certain parts of the lake between May and September, and anglers have marked-out fishing spots around the lake's 2.5km circumference. Lifeguards are on duty during opening hours. There's also a separate duck pond, and a plethora of information about the area's biosphere and protected animals.
✉ **Grenzweg, Bürgel (Offenbach)**
Mainkur **11, 12, Alt Fechenheim**
🕘 **May-Sept 8am-8pm**

Stadionbad This is Frankfurt's newest outdoor swimming pool – one look at the slides, water cannons and waterfalls is evidence. On really hot days, you'll probably only get towel room on the grass. This is a place to avoid if you're claustrophobic, but pile on in if you're a 'people' person.
✉ **Mörfelder Landstr 362, Niederrad**
☎ **67 80 41 54** **19, Stadion** **61** 🕘 **May-Aug 8am-8pm** $ **DM8/4**

out & about

WALKING TOURS

Wallanlage Wander

The *Wallanlage* marks the site of the former city walls, demolished in 1805. The surrounding moat was later closed over and landscaped, creating a green belt around the city centre.

Start at the baroque Hauptwache **(1)**, then for a contrast head for the 298m Commerzbank building **(2)** at Kaiserplatz and the European Central Bank building **(3)** on the corner of Neue Mainzer Strasse and Kaiserstrasse. Proceed to the Gallusanlage, where a statue of Goethe **(4)** looks condescendingly upon shutter-clicking tourists.

Turn right into the park towards the mirrored towers of Deutsche Bank **(5)**, passing the sculpture *Den Opfern* **(6)**, a WWI memorial. At Taunustor is the masterful Japan Center **(7)**, dwarfed by the 200m Main Tower **(8)**. Turn right at the top of the Taunusanlage across Junghofstrasse towards the Alte Oper **(9)**, past the 1961 Marshall fountain **(10)**, dedicated to the architect of the German economic miracle. Cross Opernplatz towards Bockenheimer Anlage, and pause at the pond **(11)**. Behind the Hilton, the classical Niebbiensches Gartenhaus **(12)** hosts art exhibitions.

Follow the subway route to Eschenheimer Tor **(13)**, the only intact city gate. Proceed towards Friedberger Anlage, past Bethmann Park **(14)**, to the Uhrtürmchen clock tower **(15)** in front of the zoo **(16)**. Follow the Obermainanlage to the river bank and the Portikus art gallery **(17)**, through the former city library's facade. Walk along the bank to the Eiserner Steg bridge **(18)** then north past the Römerberg **(19)** to Paulsplatz **(20)** for a well-earned cappuccino.

SIGHTS & HIGHLIGHTS

Hauptwache (p. 33)
Alte Oper (p. 30 & 96)
Eschenheimer Tor (p. 32)
Bethmann Park (p. 39)
Zoo (p. 29)
Römerberg (p. 24)
Paulsplatz (p. 25)

distance 6km **duration** 3½hrs
start Ⓤ Hauptwache
end Ⓤ Römer

Main River Meander

Start at the north end of the Eiserner Steg pedestrian bridge **(1)**, strolling westward along the embankment path, where a historic steam train runs during summer.

Duck under the Untermainbrücke **(2)** toward the Nizza **(3)**. Move up to the Holbeinsteg **(4)**, the newest bridge across the Main and a perfect avenue to the majestic Städel art gallery **(5)**. For a meander through the museums, stay at street level. If it's Saturday, you're likely to hit the flea market **(6)** (8am-2pm) between the Holbeinsteg and the Eiserner Steg.

The eye-catching facade of the Museum für Kunsthandwerk **(7)** beckons in the park. A little farther along, the Strandperle bar **(8)** in the south pier of the Eiserner Steg is an example of the efforts afoot to revive the area.

Down at water level, roller-blades and motorised scooters have elbowed out the bicycle as the preferred mode of transport. Beware of the swans that home in around the island in the river at the Alte Brücke **(9)**.

Housing projects such as the one on the former slaughterhouse site **(10)** at Deutschherrnufer are making the river embankment an attractive place to live. Continue to the grassy embankment, where boathouse restaurants serve thirsty rowing-club members.

Just 500m farther along is the Gerbermühle **(11)**, your destination. Goethe frequently visited here, in love with the daughter of the aristocrat owner. Now it's one of Frankfurt's most popular beer gardens and a hotel.

SIGHTS & HIGHLIGHTS

Städelsches Kunstinstitut (p. 27)
Museum für Kunsthandwerk (p.37)
Gerbermühle (p. 72)

Martin Moos

Eiserner Steg bridge over the Main

distance 5km **duration** 3hrs
start Römer
end Kaiserlei

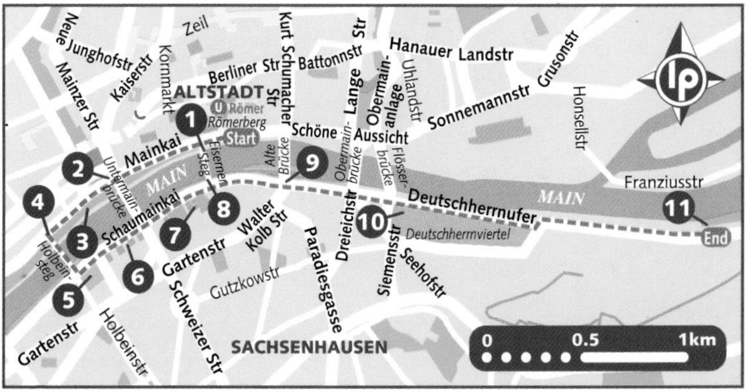

Park Promenade

From Bockenheimer Landstrasse head down Siesmayerstrasse, past the Palmengarten (botanic garden) **(1)**. Cross into Grüneburgpark **(2)**, Frankfurt's largest public park, taking the path to the left, where you'll eventually pass the Greek Orthodox Church **(3)**. Stop for a coffee at the nearby pavilion.

After completing the full circle, exit the park at Fürstenbergerstrasse, and turn left. Continue past the imposing IG Farben building **(4)**, which houses part of Frankfurt's university. Stay on Fürstenbergerstrasse until you reach Hansaallee. Turn left here, then right into Holzhausenstrasse, the more affluent part of Nordend known locally as *Dichterviertel*, or 'poet's corner'.

Enter the picturesque Holzhausenpark **(5)** at Hammanstrasse. Take the diagonal route that swings to the left around the moated baroque castle Holzhausenschlösschen **(6)**, built in 1729. Pause for reflection at the park benches at the moat.

Walk along wide Kastanienallee, named after the chestnut trees that adorn it, before turning left onto Paul-Hindemith-Anlage, and proceed to Eckenheimer Landstrasse. North of here, on the left, is the Deutsche Bibliothek **(7)**, the striking national library.

Cross at the pedestrian lights at Nibelungenallee towards the main gate of the Hauptfriedhof **(8)**, the city cemetery, where philosophers Arthur Schopenhauer and Theodor Adorno, and the children's author Heinrich Hoffmann, are buried. The Jewish graveyard on Ratbeilstrasse holds members of the distinguished Rothschild family.

SIGHTS & HIGHLIGHTS

Palmengarten & Grüneburgpark (p. 23)
IG Farbenhaus building (p. 33)
Holzhausenschlösschen (p. 22)
Deutsche Bibliothek (p. 22)
Hauptfriedhof (p. 22)

distance 5km **duration** 3½hrs
start Ⓤ Westend
end Ⓤ Hauptfriedhof

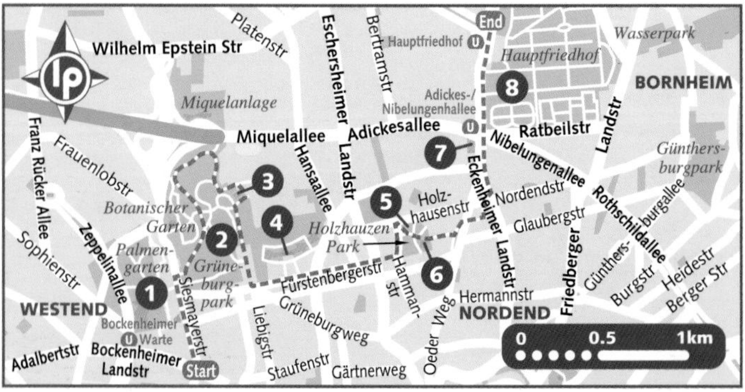

Forest Fossick

This beautful forest walk is a real get-away-from-it-all, just a 10-minute tram ride from the centre. Take the No 14 tram from Südbahnhof to Neu-Isenburg and get off at Oberschweinstiege **(1)** in the Stadtwald. Turn left into the forest along Oberschweinstiegschneise, marked on a wooden sign nailed to a tree. After about 50m, take a diagonal right along a beaten track towards the Jacobiweiher **(2)**, a mini-lake, complete with ducks to feed.

Follow the path to the left until you reach a walkway leading to the Gasthaus Oberschweinstiege **(3)**, a giant garden restaurant that serves *Naturtrübes Pils*, unfiltered pilsener beer brewed in all its natural glory.

Follow the blue-white-and-green bicycle route sign pointing to Goetheturm, 3.2km away. Before reaching the main Frankfurt to Neu-Isenburg road (Darmstädter Landstrasse), take the path to the right leading up to a wooden-sheltered bridge. At the other side, go through the wooden gate and walk straight ahead along the horse-riding path for about 1km.

SIGHTS & HIGHLIGHTS

Jacobiweiher
Goetheturm (p. 32)
Waldspielpark (p. 43)

Turn right at the junction, and take the first main path to the left, crossing the Babenhäuser Landstrasse. Go straight ahead over one path, and Wendelsweg, to the second path, where a sign points left to Goetheturm.

The Goetheturm **(4)** is a 43.3m-high wooden tower. The children's playground at the tower is a delight, but a tame tea party compared to the nearby Waldspielpark Scheerwald **(5)**, a little farther east along the path near Buchrainstrasse at the edge of the suburb of Oberrad.

(Note that, while the Stadtwald is popular with families, cyclists, joggers and romantics, it's inadvisable to be there after dusk falls. Apart from the dangers of getting lost, a number of attacks have been reported there in the past.)

distance 5.5km **duration** 3½hrs
start tram 14, Oberschweinstiege
end bus 36, Goetheturm

EXCURSIONS

Wiesbaden (5, C4)

This spa town experienced its high point at the turn of the 20th century when Europe's rich came to be treated for rheumatic and heart afflictions, or simply to wallow in the luxury of its springs and baths and stroll its promenades.

Spend a day walking in their footsteps, starting with a visit to the historic **Kaiser-Friedrich Therme**, an exquisite Roman-style bathing facility served by the *Adlerquelle*, or Eagle Spring. Lie on the warm sand of the sand bath, or sit in the stone steam bath where an antique metal contraption fires up small rocks before lowering them to sizzle in the water.

Spoil yourself in the giant whirlpools, the Finnish sauna or the Roman-Irish steam bath; and torture yourself under the 'tropical ice-rain' shower. Prepare for a culture shock: Germans like to bare all, so textile-free bathing is the done thing.

Leave time for a visit to the **Kurpark**, where jazz bands play on Sunday mornings in summer. Russian author Fyodor Dostoevsky was a regular visitor to the casino here, which inspired his novel *The Gambler*. Relaxed shopping on the **Wilhelmstrasse** makes a welcome change from battling through Frankfurt's Zeil.

The No 1 bus (from opposite the main exit at Wiesbaden Hauptbahnhof) climbs to the delightful hilltop park **Neroberg**, for a panorama of the town perched on the banks of the Rhine. From April to October, a water-driven tram goes from the foot of the Neroberg to the summit. The **Opelbad** Art Deco open-air swimming pool, below the Neroberg, is a big attraction.

During May the town hosts the International Festival of Music, Ballet & Drama.

INFORMATION

40km west of Frankfurt
duration: day

- S1, S8, or regular train from Frankfurt Hauptbahnhof
- www.english.wiesbaden.de
- Tourist Information, Marktstr 6, ☎ 0611-17 29 780; **Kaiser-Friedrich Therme** ☎ 0611-17 29 660
- 10am-10pm (Fri to midnight); Tues women's day, Wed men's day
- DM31.50 for 4hrs bathing; bathrobe/towel hire DM15/7.50

Angela Cullen

Tram ascending the Neroberg

Darmstadt Mathildenhöhe (5, E7)

Inspired by a trip to England in the 1890s, Grand Duke Ernst Ludwig of Hessen-Darmstadt founded the Mathildenhöhe artists' colony in Darmstadt's north-east. He invited renowned European artists, including Joseph Maria Olbrich and Peter Behrens, to participate in his project to revolutionise living culture. Their works, making decorative art out of everyday objects, formed the core of the German *Jugendstil* art movement and influenced the French Art Deco movement.

During the colony's 15 year existence – 1899-1914 – the artists designed and furnished their houses, and the surrounding complex, and held 4 world exhibitions.

Many of their works are displayed in the **Museum Künstlerkolonie**. The artists' houses are now private homes, but a guided tour (11.30am on the first Sunday of each month) includes a visit to one of them. Take a walk around the streets below the museum to see the magnificent exteriors of their houses.

INFORMATION

30km south of Frankfurt
duration: half-day

- S3 to Darmstadt, or RE train from Frankfurt Hauptbahnhof. From Darmstadt Hauptbahnhof, east exit, bus D to Woog or Ostbahnhof, or bus F to Lucasweg Mathildenhöhe (one-way DM10.50 Frankfurt-Darmstadt train ticket includes bus trip; buy return ticket from bus driver)
- ✉ Mathildenhöhe, Alexandraweg/Bauhausweg, Darmstadt
- ⓘ guided tours in English: book at tourist office ☎ 06151-13 20 79
- museum & tower Tues-Sun 10am-5pm; church daily 8.30am-5pm
- $ gallery & museum DM5 each or DM7 for both; church DM1.50 donation
- ✕ Atelier restaurant

Changing art exhibitions are held in the neighbouring gallery, **Ausstellungsgebäude Mathildenhöhe**. The landmark 5-fingered **Hochzeitsturm**, a 48m tower designed by Olbrich, was presented to the city in 1905 by Ernst Ludwig to mark his marriage.

The Russian Orthodox church **St Maria Magdalena** is open to visitors.

Martin Moos

The artists' colony, framed by the Hochzeitsturm and the Russian Orthodox church

Saalburg (5, A6)

The ancient Roman site at Saalburg gives a fascinating glimpse of life in a Roman fort around the 2nd century AD. The main attraction is the reconstruction (completed 1898-1907) of a **fortress** which housed a unit of around 500 soldiers. You can also explore the excavated **ruins** of other original buildings (houses, baths, wells etc) and walk on a section of the original *Limes*, a stone wall which marked the northern boundary of the Roman Empire.

In the *Horreum* (the former granary), the **museum** displays tools, clothing, ornaments and other relics recovered from the area. Many of these were preserved in the damp mud in the compound's many wells. Other exhibits show the Romans were purveyors of foodstuffs, condiments and spices millennia before the word 'globalisation' entered our vocabulary.

The exhibits are labelled in German but an English booklet is available (DM3.50).

INFORMATION

25km north of Frankfurt
duration: half-day
- S5 to Bad Homburg, then bus 5 to Saalburg (departs Bad Homburg every 2hrs 9.50am-5.50pm)
- Saalburg-Kastell, Bad Homburg
- 06172-17 81 10
- 8am-5pm
- DM5
- Gasthaus Saalburg

Martin Moos

'Halt! Do you have your ticket?'

Martin Moos

Saalburg's reconstructed Roman fortress

Rheingau Wine Region (5, D2)

Germany may be a major export nation, but it sure doesn't like to part with its wines. Thus, it may be that your only experience of German wines has been a violent one with *Liebfraumilch* or Blue Nun. This gap in your education can easily be corrected with a trip to the compact **Rheingau** wine region, known for its fragrant and lively rieslings and the home of some of the world's most long-established wine-growing families.

INFORMATION

100km west of Frankfurt
duration: day
train to Rüdesheim takes 1½hrs (some go direct, others require changing at Wiesbaden)
ⓘ Rüdesheim tourist office
☎ 06722-29 62

The Rheingau landscape, a scenic patchwork of vineyards clinging to the hillsides above the Rhine River, is dotted with medieval towns and castles. The **Rheingau Riesling Route** stretches roughly between the towns of Eltville and Lorch on the Rhine, and is marked by signs bearing a Roman goblet. The **Rheingauer Rieslingpfad** is a well-marked 100km hiking trail through the region's highlands and lowlands. There are plenty of vintner-cum-guesthouses along the way offering overnight accommodation.

Wine-growers traditionally open their cellars in April and September for impromptu tastings. Many open a *Strausswirtschaft* (temporary wine bar) for a few weeks in spring and autumn. They traditionally hang out a *Strauss* (a wreath with a glass in it) to attract custom.

If you're travelling by car, stop at the beautiful estates of **Schloss Johannisberg** and **Schloss Vollrads**, and the towns of **Hallgarten** and **Hattenheim**. If time is precious and you're limited to trains, the towns of **Rüdesheim** and **Assmannshausen** are logical stops, but overrun by tourists. Both are also boarding points for boat cruises downriver to the legendary **Loreley** rock and picturesque **St Goarshausen**.

David Peevers

Another bumper vintage in the making

ORGANISED TOURS

Frankfurt is compact enough to explore on foot, or there are plenty of bus tours on offer. For something different, hop on a bike or boat, or take a tour beyond the city centre.

BICYCLE TOURS

Allgemeiner Deutsche Fahrrad-Club (2, B13)
The bicycle club organises cycling tours around the region and farther afield. Visit the Infoshop to find out more.
✉ Berger Str 108-110, Bornheim ☎ 499 01 00 ⌚ Infoshop open Mon-Fri 5.15-7pm, Sat 11am-1pm $ free

RIVER TOURS

Primus Linie/ Wikinger Linie
(2, H8) Departing from the Eiserner Steg bridge, explore the Main River by boat on a 1½hr tour, from the Gerbermühle in the east to the barge locks at Griesheim in the west. Look out for the museums precinct on the south bank, and great views of Frankfurt's skyline.
✉ Eiserner Steg, Untermainkai ☎ 133 83 70 ⌚ Sun & holidays every half-hr $ DM12

Ornamented old meets needle-like new in the Münchener Strasse neighbourhood.

Martin Moos

BUS & WALKING TOURS

Frankfurt City Tour
(5, C6) Private tours of the historic old town and banking district, with stops for camera clicking. English-speaking guides are available. Tours start and end at the airport and last around 2½hrs; they require a minimum of 2 people.
✉ depart from airport ☎ 62 22 95 ⌚ daily 7.45 & 10.45am, 1.45 & 4.45pm $ DM55 per person (children under 10 free); credit cards accepted

Freundeskreis Liebenswertes Frankfurt (2, F7)
The 'Circle of Friends' are a group of Frankfurters who volunteer to show people around the city they love. It can take days to arrange a tour. Groups meet at the clock at the Hauptwache.
✉ depart from Hauptwache ☎ 47 93 61, 74 85 82 $ free

Kulturothek (3, A2)
This private tour company offers creative walking and bus tours that claim to reveal the undiscovered side of Frankfurt. It holds 1½hr tours in German most Sundays at 2pm. English-speaking guides

are available for 2½hrs for groups.
✉ **An der Kleinmarkthalle 7 ☎ 28 10 10 ⓢ DM198 flat rate for group of 25 or less**

Statt-Reisen Frankfurt (3, C2)
This nonprofit group offers historical walking tours through the city centre. Groups meet outside the Historisches Museum on Römerberg.
✉ **Ringelstr 50, Bornheim ☎ 46 33 59 ⓢ DM200 flat rate for group of 16-20 people**

Tourismus & Congress GmbH
(3, C2) The tourist office runs a 2½hr tour that manages to pack in the Römerberg, Goethe-Haus, Sachsenhausen, a glimpse through Westend – including the IG Farben building and Palmengarten – the Bahnhofsviertel and Bockenheim.

It also offers thematic tours such as Architectural Frankfurt, the banking district, Jewish Frankfurt and a walk in Goethe's footsteps. Go with a group to make the most of the DM100 flat rate for the first 2hrs.
✉ **Tourist Info Römer, Römerberg 27 ☎ 21 23 89 53 🕘 Apr-Oct: 10am & 2pm; Nov-Mar: 2pm ⓢ 2½hr tour DM44 per person; thematic tour DM100 (group)**

TOURS BEYOND THE CITY

Primus Linie/ Wikinger Linie
(2, H8) See the Rhine-Main region from the rivers that define it. This outfit offers boat trips to the Main River towns of Seligenstadt, Aschaffenburg and Miltenberg to the east; and along the Rhine to Rüdesheim, Assmannshausen and St Goar. In July, don't miss the chance to view the Rhine in Flames festival from the water.
✉ **Eiserner Steg, Untermainkai ☎ 133 83 70 ⓢ varies**

Tourismus & Congress GmbH
(3, C2) Out-of-town bus tours to Höchst, Heidelberg, the Taunus Hills and the Rheingau wine region are available. The tours can be tailored to group requests.
✉ **Tourist Info Römer, Römerberg 27 ☎ 21 23 89 53 ⓢ varies**

DIY Bike Touring

Armed with a good map, you can organise your own cycling tour. The Rhine-Main region is well served by cycling routes, marked by wooden signposts, or the characteristic blue and green signs of the *Grüngürtel* ('green belt').

Two routes worth trying are the trail from Frankfurt to Wiesbaden (55km) through the beautiful towns of Flörsheim and Hochheim – home of the famous Hochheimer wine – or eastwards along the Main's south bank to Seligenstadt (35km). The best maps are put out by the Umlandverband Frankfurt and include train links and tourist tips (available at most good bookshops).

Holy Frankfurt!

Pick up a leaflet at any inner city church (eg Katharinenkirche) and make your own tour of 8 churches around the Römerberg and Sachsenhausen. Allow about an hour.

Martin Moos

Kaiserdom cathedral

shopping

Like many aspects of Frankfurt, finding the interesting side to shopping takes some detective work. That's not to say that good shopping can't be found. If it's high-quality electronics or sports equipment you want, Frankfurt will have it. The same goes for big-name European fashion. Germans don't like to leave home without being dressed to the nines, even if it's only to go window-shopping on Sunday afternoon, which they do frequently. There's also a strong youth culture and a prevalent music scene. And for the best in European wines, cheeses, sausage and bread, you need look no further.

Opening hours are restricted to 8am-8pm Monday to Friday and 8am-4pm on Saturday, but the farther away from the Zeil you go, the earlier the shops are likely to close.

A law limiting discounting means few bargain-basement prices. Expect to pay a small fortune for labels and designer goods, but competitive prices for electronics and photographic equipment. The German knack for inspiring gifts (and gift-wrapping) and mouth-watering bread make a visit to a gift shop and a bakery an absolute must. And should the chance to test-drive a Porsche or a Daimler present itself, don't turn it down.

Tax-Free Shopping

Most goods in Germany carry a 16% Value Added Tax, which non-EU nationals can partly reclaim upon departure. Shops that carry the 'Tax-Free Shopping' sign will have Global Refund Cheques, which you present to customs along with your purchases for validation. Eligible shoppers can claim a refund of up to 11% from Cash Refund Offices located at the Reisebank at Frankfurt Hauptbahnhof, the IWS Change, Kaiserstrasse 81, or at a number of locations at the airport.

Shopping Districts

For pure mainstream, stick with the **Zeil**, which links the Hauptwache and the Konstablerwache. It's actually Germany's busiest shopping street, but often it just means queue after queue. Sachsenhausen's **Schweizer Strasse** is a wonderful mix of boutiques, delis and art shops with the odd cafe or gelateria. Bornheim's **Berger Strasse** is good for young fashion, books, electrical goods, bicycles and knick-knacks. Bockenheim's villagey **Leipziger Strasse** is a bustling, cobblestoned street with food markets, quirky bakeries, wine stores and a bountiful mall. Nordend's **Oeder Weg** is health-minded with organic fruit and vegetable stores and outdoor pursuits outlets, while Ostend's **Hanauer Landstrasse** specialises in interior decor, cars...and busy traffic. **Kaiserstrasse** has many tax-free stores stocking electronics, photographic equipment, hi-fi and porcelain.

Martin Moos

Smile as you spend – Zeil shopping strip

DEPARTMENT STORES & SHOPPING MALLS

Arabella Ladengalerie (2, E9)
Indian, Chinese and Japanese restaurants rub shoulders with a paint shop, a quirky ornament shop and some neat little cafes.
✉ **Grosse Friedberger Str** Ⓤ **Konstablerwache** 🕘 **Mon-Fri 9.30am-8pm, Sat 9am-4pm**

Fressgasse-Passage (2, E6) For the expats among you, the deli at the corner of this shopping arcade and throughway from Fressgasse to Goethestrasse sells massive bars of Cadbury's for less than DM5. The tea shop is one you could find on the *Schnoor* in Bremen.
✉ **Grosse Bockenheimer Str** Ⓤ **Hauptwache; Alte Oper** 🕘 **Mon-Fri 9.30am-8pm, Sat 9am-4pm**

Hauptwache Passage (2, E7) Roller-bladers and snowboarders unite at Rail Slide. Do the full circle around the passageway underneath the Hauptwache to find nooks and crannies full of fruit and vegetable markets, fast-food takeaways, the best (English-language) card shop in town, and quality shoe shops.
✉ **Hauptwache B-Ebene,** Ⓤ **Hauptwache** 🕘 **Mon-Fri 9.30am-8pm, Sat 9am-4pm**

Hertie (2, E9)
This Zeil landmark is where you'll unexpectedly find the city's main post office, and there's a fantastic selection of international foodstuffs in the basement. It stocks everything from cosmetics to suitcases.
✉ **Zeil 90** ☎ **92 90 50** Ⓤ **Konstablerwache** 🕘 **Mon-Fri 9.30am-8pm, Sat 9am-4pm**

Kaufhof (2, E7)
The multistorey Kaufhof is part of a major German retail chain, and stocks everything imaginable, at bargain prices. There's one in every town.
✉ **Zeil 116-126** ☎ **219 10** Ⓤ **Hauptwache** 🕘 **Mon-Fri 9.30am-8pm, Sat 9am-4pm**

Off-Zeil

A forage in the streets around or near the Zeil can turn up some treats, including the following.

Grosse Eschenheimer Strasse, Schillerstrasse, Stiftstrasse – wacky shoes, space-age clothing, expensive kitchenware

Steinweg, Rossmarkt – designer fashion, jewellery

Töngesgasse, Berliner Strasse – the home of interior design, street-cred clothing

Braubachstrasse, Saalgasse – art galleries galore

Fahrgasse – a haven for antique-lovers

Domstrasse – interior design, art books

Goethestrasse – high-class fashion boutiques (enter them in anything less than Helmut Lang, and you will probably be eyed for shop-lifting)

Fressgasse – lingerie, classic cuts, inspiring cheese-and-wine and gift stores

Grüneburgweg, Kronberger Strasse (Westend) – pockets of exclusive interior design, fashion outlets

Martin Moos

The hip Delirium clothes shop

Ladengalerie Bockenheimer Warte
(4, A4) You'll find the best graphic art posters, quirky interior design and cheap CDs and books at this engaging Bockenheim arcade.
✉ **Leipziger Str/Adalbertstr, Bockenheim**
Ⓤ Bockenheimer Warte **🚊 16** 🕘 **Mon-Fri 9.30am-8pm, Sat 9am-4pm**

Nordwestzentrum
This shopping centre can be a wind-trap, but it has fashion boutiques without queues, good Asian shops and one of the cheapest outlets around for ski gear. While you're there visit the Titus Thermen swimming pool, leisure and sauna complex. It's out of town, but easy to get to on the U1 line.
✉ **Limescorso, Nordweststadt**
☎ **58 09 02**
Ⓤ Nordwestzentrum
🕘 **Mon-Fri 9.30am-8pm, Sat 9am-4pm**

It's all there at the Zeilgalerie shopping mall.

Sandhofpassage
(3, B2) A favourite shopping spot among the gay community with the flamboyant Dom interior design store, the delightful Cafe Lilliput and hi-fi stores to die for.
✉ **Neue Kräme 29**
Ⓤ Hauptwache
🕘 **Mon-Fri 9.30am-8pm, Sat 9am-4pm**

Schiller-Passage
(2, E7) Hidden behind the stock exchange, this delightful mini-mall will surprise you with smart art, avant-garde ladies' fashion and an esoteric bookshop.
✉ **Rahmhofstr 2**
Ⓤ Hauptwache
🕘 **Mon-Fri 9.30am-8pm, Sat 9am-4pm**

Steinweg-Passage
(2, F7) This mini-mall can claim one of the city's best Thai restaurants and an excellent toy shop as well as tea for two thousand, and men's underwear (yes, CK makes an appearance).
✉ **Steinweg**
Ⓤ Hauptwache
🕘 **Mon-Fri 9.30am-8pm, Sat 9am-4pm**

Zeilgalerie (2, E8)
This funky, open-plan structure ribbed with escalators and tubes is the city's most progressive shopping mall. It's designed for browsing; an hour wandering down the spiral of fashion stores, trendy cafes, art shops and music outlets will be an hour (and possibly a wallet) well spent.
✉ **Zeil 112-114**
☎ **920 73 40**
Ⓤ Hauptwache
🕘 **Mon-Fri 9.30am-8pm, Sat 9am-4pm**

MARKETS

Farmers from outlying regions come into town to sell their fresh produce at a number of excellent food markets around town. Time it right and you could go to a different one almost every day of the week.

Bockenheimer Wochenmarkt (4, A5)
Organic farmers sell quality meat, fresh vegetables and dairy products. There's also every type of bread imaginable, including the most exquisite onion bread in the universe.
✉ **Bockenheimer Warte, Bockenheim** Ⓤ **Bockenheimer Warte** 🚊 **16**
🕘 **Thurs 8am-6pm**

Bornheimer Wochenmarkt (2, A15)
So good they do it twice a week! Fresh flowers for next to nothing. Don't buy your cheese anywhere else. Out of an excellent choice, this fresh fruit and vegetable market is many people's favourite.
✉ **Marktplatz/Am Uhrtürmchen, Bornheim**
Ⓤ **Bornheim Mitte**
🚊 **12** 🕘 **Wed 8am-6pm, Sat 8am-2pm**

Discount-Zentrale
(2, K10) It's too neat to be called a jumble sale, perhaps a tidy flea market would be a better description. This is your chance to find an old Villeroy & Boch dinner or coffee service.
✉ **Textorstr 26, Sachsenhausen** ☎ **96 20 15 28** Ⓤ **Lokalbahnhof**
🚊 **14-16** 🕘 **Mon-Fri 1-7pm, Sat 10am-4pm**

Flohmarkt Sachsenhausen
(2, J6-7) Some narky residents have been trying to move the Sachsenhausen flea market away from its location on the south bank for years, but this Frankfurt institution has a keen survival instinct, and a mass of supporters. It's a great spot to pick up a cheap old bicycle, antique furniture and chess sets.
✉ **Am Schaumainkai, Sachsenhausen**
Ⓤ **Römer; Schweizer Platz** 🚌 **46**
🕘 **Sat 9am-2pm**

Kleinmarkthalle
(3, A3) This food-market hall is a Frankfurt institution with over 50 stands selling everything from fresh fruit and vegetables to marinated olives and herbs, and flower bulbs. Be sure to try a Gref Völsings Rindswurst, or beef sausage, also a Frankfurt institution.
✉ **Hasengasse 5-7**
☎ **21 23 36 96**
Ⓤ **Hauptwache; Römer**
🕘 **Mon-Fri 7.30am-6pm, Sat 7.30am-3pm**

Konstablerwache
(2, E9) This market is the only thing that brings the Konstablerwache to life once a week. There's honey, fresh from the beehive, fresh and cooked meats, and home-made applewine.
✉ **Konstablerwache**
Ⓤ **Konstablerwache**
🕘 **Sat 8am-4pm**

Schillerstrassen Markt (2, E7)
If it's Friday, it must be Schillerstrasse, wonderful for olives, cheese, grilled chicken and wine.
✉ **Schillerstr**
Ⓤ **Hauptwache** 🕘 **Fri 8am-6.30pm**

Souk Kunsthandwerk Karim Semmar
(2, F10) With valuable Moroccan artwork and all the charm of a souk, this is more than just a market. Semmar sells to a sophisticated clientele.
✉ **Battonstr 4-8**
☎ **28 56 30**
Ⓤ **Konstablerwache**
🚊 **11, Börneplatz**
🕘 **Mon-Fri 11am-7pm, Sat 10am-4pm**

Martin Moos

Fruit stall, Hauptwache Passage

CLOTHING & JEWELLERY

58's Buy Heidt (2, C3) It pays to move off the beaten track, when you discover a fashion boutique of this quality. It stocks international designers such as Yohji Yamamito, Helmut Lang and Ann Demeulemeester, as well as Stone Island, Jil Sander and Dolce & Gabbana. No wonder *GQ* and *Vogue* dropped in for a closer look.
✉ **Kronberger Str 19, Westend ☎ 72 55 35 Ⓤ Westend ⏲ Mon-Wed 10am-6.30pm, Thurs-Fri 11am-8pm, Sat 11am-4pm**

Akris (2, E6) This acclaimed Swiss fashion house caters for the elegant businesswoman. Classic cuts in luxurious surrounds.
✉ **Grosse Bockenheimer Str 13 ☎ 21 99 67 00 Ⓤ Hauptwache ⏲ Mon-Fri 10am-7pm, Sat 10am-4pm**

Albrecht Ollendiek (3, C3) Albrecht is Frankfurt's internationally best-known fashion designer. The window displays of flamboyant ball gowns and theatre costumes are only one aspect of his versatility. And he's in the right environment to stimulate his creativity: the Saalgasse is a unique display of funky architecture by local designers.
✉ **Saalgasse 10 ☎ 91 39 92 31 Ⓤ Römer ⏲ Mon-Fri 3-6.30pm, Sat 10am-2pm**

Burresi Occasioni (2, B5) Stepping out in Westend is this highly popular Italian shoe outlet with discount designer shoes. It's a real find.
✉ **Grüneburgweg 12, Westend ☎ 59 03 59 Ⓤ Grüneburgweg ⏲ Mon-Fri 9.30am-6.30pm (closed Thurs 2-3pm), Sat 9.30am-2pm**

Carl Theobald (2, E6) Some of the antique furniture in this goldsmith's could be as old as the establishment itself (over 250 years). Frankfurt's most respected address for the older generation also attracts a curious younger crowd. You'll find white gold and South Pacific pearls.
✉ **Rathenauplatz 2-8 ☎ 28 20 57 Ⓤ Hauptwache ⏲ Mon-Fri 10am-7pm, Sat 10am-4pm**

Cascoon (2, C11) Way-out fashion and wacky shoes typical of the unimpressionable Berger Strasse. The 70s revisited in 2 separate locations.
✉ **Berger Str 54 & 63, Bornheim/Nordend ☎ 499 06 04 Ⓤ Merianplatz ⏲ Mon-Fri 10am-7.30pm, Sat 10am-4pm**

Delirium (3, A2) Techno labels such as Evisu Genes and Combo are the hallmarks of this brash off-Zeil outfit. This is also the No 1 address for the latest techno and house music releases.
✉ **Töngesgasse 42 ☎ 297 71 16 Ⓤ Hauptwache ⏲ Mon-Fri 11am-7pm, Sat 10am-4pm**

Ehinger-Schwarz (2, E5) Goethestrasse neighbours Cartier and Tiffany take care of the classics, allowing upstarts like this to spread their wings with experimental jewellery. Its patented Charlotte and Tipin ranges cleverly include replaceable bits to create not one but several decorative pieces.
✉ **Goethestr 18 ☎ 92 91 91 82 Ⓤ Alte Oper ⏲ Mon-Fri 10am-7pm, Sat 10am-4pm**

Escape Futura (3, B1) Artwork for feet. Designer shoes by Free Lance, David Ackermann and Kelian in a futuristic setting, and custom-made items.
✉ **Sandgasse 4 ☎ 13 37 71 07 Ⓤ Hauptwache ⏲ Mon-Fri 10.30am-8pm, Sat 10am-4pm**

Factory Outlet (1, F10) Get your Ralph Laurens and Helmut Langs

Seasonal Sales

Steep discounts can be had at the annual *Winter-* and *Sommerschlussverkäufe* sales held for 2 weeks at the end of January/beginning of February, and July/August, respectively. Nonmaterialists can pick up last year's ski models or last season's fashions for as little as half-price.

cheaper than anywhere else. There's also Dolce & Gabbana and Sergio Rossa as well as other European designers.
Hanauer Landstr 155, Ostend 43 05 71 44 11, Schwedlerstr Mon-Fri 10am-8pm, Sat 9am-4pm

Marc O' Polo (2, F7) Measuring 600 sq m, this is Europe's largest Marc O' Polo outlet. A cool white decor and plenty of strolling room; gents' gear downstairs.
Steinweg 9
21 99 70 26
Hauptwache
Mon-Fri 10am-8pm, Sat 10am-4pm

May & Edlich (2, F7) It it's Armani you're seeking, then look no further. Separate ladies' and gents' outlets for exclusive European designer wear.
Steinweg 7
28 45 83
Hauptwache
Mon-Fri 10am-8pm, Sat 9.30am-4pm

Peek & Cloppenburg (2, E9) The most trusted name on the Zeil. This gigantic clothing store on 4 levels will have what you want. And just when you think it's getting too conservative, the basement floor throws up a selection of hip young fashion: Esprit, Joop, Marc O' Polo.
Zeil 71-75
29 89 50
Konstablerwache
Mon-Fri 10am-8pm, Sat 9.30am-4pm

Ria Leslau (2, E6) It's the funky purple, bubbly walls that grab you when you enter this tiny jeweller's. Ria's original designs have become a popular attraction in the few years she's been here. This is no ordinary jewellery and accessory outlet.
Hochstr 53
28 71 87 Alte Oper Mon-Fri 11am-7pm, Sat 11am-4pm

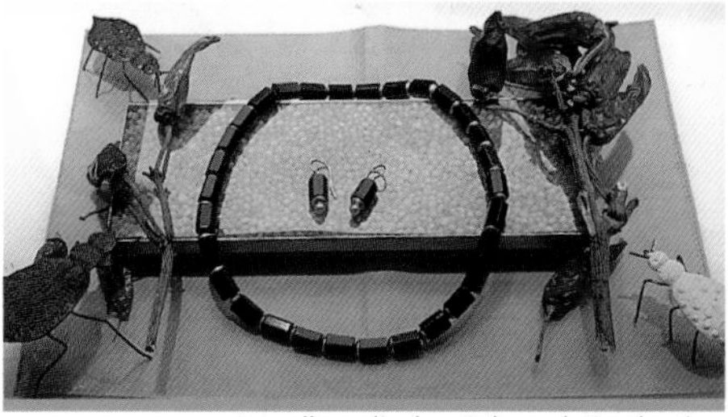
Martin Moos
Jewellery display, Schmuck Production

Schmuck Production (2, E8) Gold, platinum and precious stones are the core ingredients for expensive but highly individual designs from local goldsmith Irene Chiara Klar.
Stiftstr 23
29 68 48
Eschenheimer Tor
Tues-Fri 11am-7pm, Sat 11am-3pm

Stoffwechsel (2, D7) Hip casuals from as-yet unknown international designers. Check out neighbouring boutiques that have gravitated to this corner of town in recent years.
Stiftstr 36
297 78 72
Eschenheimer Tor
Mon-Fri 11am-8pm, Sat 12-4pm

Time Office (1, F10) A bring-and-buy outlet for designer steel objects and old watches. It deals in Rolex, Breitling, IWC, Omega, Heuer and Tudor timepieces, and also does valuations and repairs. It's off the beaten track but is worth the venture.
Hanauer Landstr 133, Ostend
94 41 16 67
11, Schwedlerstr
Tues-Fri 10am-2pm, 3-7pm, Sat 11am-2pm

Martin Moos
Finds for every fashion follower

OUTDOOR GEAR

Alpinsport (2, E9)
If you wait till summer you can pick up last year's skis and boots at a discount. Big Foot and carvers are available.
✉ **Grosse Friedberger Str 18-20**
☎ **913 31 40**
Konstablerwache
🕘 **Mon-Wed 11am-7pm, Thurs-Fri 10am-7.30pm, Sat 9.30am-4pm**

Ben Bike/McTrek
(4, C3) This outdoor store specialises in seconds and outdated models, sold at big discounts. It stocks professional bikes and cycling gear, waterproofs, fleeces, rucksacks and climbing boots.
✉ **Hamburger Allee 49-53, Bockenheim**
☎ **97 99 20 20**
Westbahnhof
🕘 **Mon-Fri 10am-7pm, Sat 10am-4pm**

Sine (2, B7)
This is Frankfurt's top address for outdoor gear including Gore-Tex, Jack Wolfskin, Fjäll Räven and Eagle Creek. A few doors down, a sister outlet focuses on rucksacks and camping gear.
✉ **Oeder Weg 43, Nordend** ☎ **55 22 33**
Eschenheimer Tor
🕘 **Mon-Fri 10am-8pm, Sat 9am-4pm**

Topsport (2, F7)
Designer-wear and equipment for snowboarders. Chiemsee and Fire & Ice sell like hotcakes, but Burton is probably the name most shoppers are here for.
✉ **Kl Hirschgraben 3-7**
☎ **59 07 37**
Hauptwache
🕘 **Mon-Fri 11am-7pm, Sat 10am-3pm**

FOR CHILDREN

Hanne Kley (2, F7)
It's hugely expensive, but your kids will love it! The expertly crafted wooden toys are more like collectors' items than playthings that mightn't last a day at home. The kiddies' clothes are also Sunday-best.
✉ **Rossmarkt 12, Steinweg-Passage**
☎ **28 48 22**
Hauptwache
🕘 **Mon-Fri 10am-6.30pm, Sat 10am-4pm**

Martin Moos

Children's heaven at Hanne Kley

Kinderhaus Pfüller
(2, E6) If you fancy your child in Ralph Lauren, Betty Barclay and DKNY, then these 3 floors of tots' clothing and babies' things won't leave you wanting. Time it right, and you could snap them up for half-price at the sales.
✉ **Goethestr 12** ☎ **13 37 80 70** **Alte Oper; Hauptwache** 🕘 **Mon-Fri 10am-7pm, Sat 10am-4pm**

Naturino (3, B2)
Instead of a day at the zoo, why not spend time at the kiddies' shoe shop? They'll love trying on hundreds of brightly-coloured boots and shoes.
✉ **Berliner Str 44**
☎ **21 99 57 12**
Hauptwache
🕘 **Mon-Fri 10am-6pm, Sat 10am-4pm**

Ritas Puppenhaus
(1, G7) Waiting to greet you are hundreds of dolls of all shapes, sizes and prices. It's like Christmas every day.
✉ **Textorstr 83, Sachsenhausen** ☎ **61 35 47** **Schweizer Platz** 🕘 **Mon-Fri 11am-6.30pm (Thurs from noon), Sat 10am-2pm**

ARTS & ANTIQUES

Antik-Bodenheimer (2, D9) Enter the world of communication at this eccentric antique shop with its collection of old gramophones, telephones, radios, typewriters and cameras.
✉ **Rosenbergerstr 6**
☎ **28 77 95**
Konstablerwache
🕘 **Mon-Fri 10am-1pm, 3-6.30pm, Sat 10am-4pm**

Die Krauts (2, E8) The closest you'll come to seeing giant metal furniture and spine-shivering artworks like Peter Ratz and Björn Reimers' throne or spider, other than here, is in a Batman film. Smaller items include hand-shaped ashtrays or dungeon-style candlesticks. Larger items run into the megadeutschmarks.
✉ **Zeilgalerie** ☎ **29 00 01** **www.diekrauts.de** **Hauptwache**
🕘 **Mon-Fri 9.30am-8pm, Sat 9am-4pm**

Fluxus (4, A4) With probably the best selection in town of posters and prints of modern and classical artworks, this place is also known for its superb collection of old and autographed postcards (yes, even Hollywood greats!). Framing to order.
✉ **Leipzigerstr 11/ Ladengalerie Bockenheimer Warte, Bockenheim** ☎ **77 45 21** **Bockenheimer Warte** 🕘 **Mon-Fri 10am-7pm, Sat 9am-2pm**

Nuovo Design Classic (3, D5) Take a leap back in time at this nostalgic second-hand shop that

Angela Cullen

Art to die for, Die Krauts

sells furniture and classic designs of the 60s and 70s. The items are judiciously arranged in a jumbled fashion, perfect for browsing.
✉ **Fahrgasse 1**
☎ **28 39 18** **Römer**
30, 36 🕘 **Tues-Fri 3-6.30pm, Sat 12-3pm**

United World of Art (2, E6) All the art in the world, from the South Seas to Africa. This is a treasure trove of exotic art for the stay-at-home traveller.
✉ **Kaiserhofstr 4**
☎ **28 25 96** **Alte Oper; Hauptwache**
🕘 **Mon-Fri 10.30am-7pm, Sat 10am-4pm**

Vonderbank (2, E6) Two floors of oils, sculptures and graphics by Picasso, Miro, Braque, Lichtenstein, Warhol and other contemporaries. You may also come across paintings by the late environmentalist Friedensreich Hundertwasser, a painter/architect whose Hundertwasser-Haus in Vienna and his vehement views on the environment put him on the map. It also does restorations.
✉ **Goethestr 11**
☎ **91 39 98 21** **Alte Oper; Hauptwache**
🕘 **Mon-Fri 10am-7pm, Sat 10am-4pm**

Wood Store (1, C14) The focus here is on old German farmhouse furniture including wardrobes and kitchen dressers.
✉ **Cassellastr 30-32, Fechenheim** ☎ **40 80 09 19** **11, Cassellastr**
🕘 **Mon-Fri 10am-6pm, Sat 12-4pm**

Yalya (2, K9) Original furniture, sculptures, ornaments and art from Turkey and the Middle East.
✉ **Laubestr 23 (cnr of Gutzkowstr), Sachsenhausen** ☎ **70 01 90**
Schweizer Platz
🕘 **Mon-Fri 10am-7pm, Sat 11am-3pm**

Martin Moos

From the 4 corners of the globe to United World of Art

MUSIC

2001 (3, B1)
Squeezing your way through the dozens of other jazz and classical music freaks to get to your choice is part of the charm of this tiny cult CD shop. It also stocks a good selection of 60s, 70s and 80s (that obscure Thelonius Monk album you're after is bound to be here).
✉ **Kornmarkt 4 ☎ 29 15 36 Ⓜ Hauptwache ⏲ Mon-Fri 10am-8pm, Sat 10am-4pm**

Bang & Olufsen Center (2, G6)
Not to mention the masters of sound systems would be sacrilege, even if the appliances are out of many people's price range.
✉ **Friedenstr 7 ☎ 24 24 60 15 Ⓜ Willy-Brandt-Platz 🚊 11 ⏲ Mon-Fri 10am-7pm, Sat 10am-4pm**

Freebase Records
(2, C9) LPs and CDs of the 'drum & bass' kind. This is one of a number of independent music shops that make up the thriving underground music scene; also sells mixers and recording equipment.
✉ **Peterstr 2**
☎ 13 37 62 55
Ⓜ Konstablerwache
🚌 36 ⏲ Mon-Fri 11am-8pm, Sat 10am-4pm

Musikladen (2, E8)
I'll risk a bet that this is the cheapest CD shop in town, although the arrival of HMV has driven prices lower all round. It also has information on concerts and gigs.
✉ **Stiftstr 2 ☎ 28 10 28 Ⓜ Hauptwache ⏲ Mon-Fri 10am-7.30pm, Sat 10am-4pm**

Say it with Flowers

All over Germany, florists are almost as common as hairdressers. People here like to mark special occasions or even a simple dinner invitation with a bunch of flowers, and you don't have to look far to find fancy bouquets or just a simple rose to put in the mini-vase in your New Beetle car. The following florists would be strong candidates to win the *Bundesgartenschau* (German Flower Show):

Alice Im Blumenland, Arabella Ladengalerie, Konrad-Adenauer-Str 7
Blumenbinderei, Bornheimer Landstr 77, Nordend
Blumenladen Beuchert, Rathenauplatz
Power Of Flowers, Eschersheimer Landstr 13, Nordend/Westend
Stil Und Blüte, Gartenstr 24, Sachsenhausen

Oliver Strewe

Saturn Hansa
(2, A14) The 3-storey electrical goods specialist Saturn stocks everything from washing machines to professional cameras and hi-fi equipment. It also has the most comprehensive, and one of the cheapest, CD selections in Frankfurt on the top floor. The jazz and blues corner and the classical music section are impressive. Go early if you want to preview your choice at the playback counter, otherwise prepare for a long queue.
✉ **Berger Str 125-129, Bornheim ☎ 40 50 10 Ⓜ Höhenstr ⏲ Mon-Fri 9.30am-8pm, Sat 9am-4pm**

Sick Wreckords
(2, H8) With a name like that, it has to sell punk music. But this second-hand music shop also has an expert selection of funk, soul, blues and...yes, even the 60s.
✉ **Schulstr 1, Sachsenhausen ☎ 61 99 47 23 Ⓜ Südbahnhof ⏲ Tues-Fri 11am-7pm, Sat 11am-4pm**

WOM (2, E8-9)
Time was when this place ruled the roost in Frankfurt when it came to latest releases. A smart underground scene and places like Saturn Hansa and HMV have changed all that. It's still got the best playback counter in Frankfurt, though, and competitive prices.
✉ **Zeilgalerie & top flr at Hertie ☎ 920 73 30 Ⓜ Konstablerwache; Hauptwache ⏲ Mon-Fri 9.30am-8pm, Sat 9am-4pm**

BOOKS

Hugendubel (2, F7)
It's more than just a bookshop. The Hugendubel concept includes a coffee shop with superb cappuccinos and couches to sit down for a read. Cashiers on the ground floor only. The queues can get unbearable.
✉ **Steinweg 12 ☎ 29 98 20 Ⓤ Hauptwache ⌚ Mon-Fri 9.30am-8pm, Sat 9.30am-4pm**

Land in Sicht (2, B10)
This little gem doesn't stock many English-language books, but is worth mentioning as a specialist in travel literature of the intellectual kind. The name means 'land in sight'. Readings and launches are held regularly.
✉ **Rotteckstr 13, Nordend ☎ 44 30 95 🚊 12, Hessendenkmal ⌚ Mon-Fri 10am-6.30pm, Sat 10am-4pm**

Landkartenhandlung Richard Schwarz
(2, B9 & G7)
This quirky shop is stacked from floor to ceiling with maps of every country and geographic region in the world. Ordnance survey maps, geological maps, antique maps and hiking and biking maps. It's been going since the turn of the 20th century, when it was based in Berlin.
✉ **Eckenheimer Landstr 36, Nordend; Gr Hirschgraben (opp Goethe-Haus) ☎ 597 51 66; 28 72 78 Ⓤ Musterschule; Hauptwache ⌚ Mon-Fri 9am-6pm, Sat 9am-noon; Mon-Fri 9.30am-7pm, Sat 10am-4pm**

Martin Moos

Wendeltreppe bookshop

Oscar Wilde (2, D9)
With a name like this, it has to be a gay literature bookshop. There are books, magazines and comics and all sorts of helpful tips about Frankfurt's gay scene. Good English-language assortment too.
✉ **Alte Gasse 51**
☎ 28 12 60
Ⓤ Konstablerwache
⌚ Mon-Fri 11am-8pm, Sat 10am-4pm

Walther König
(3, B3) Art and architecture are the themes at this established bookshop near the Dom. There's quite a selection of books in English, although the subject matter renders language irrelevant for a lot of the books.
✉ **Domstr 6**
☎ 29 65 88 Ⓤ Römer 🚊 11 ⌚ Mon-Fri 10am-6.30pm, Sat 10am-4pm

Wendeltreppe (2, J9)
Run by 2 eccentric ladies, this bookshop sells murder and intrigue. Handcuffs and crime props are evidence that the owners just adore what they do. There are some English titles stocked.
✉ **Brückenstr 34, Sachsenhausen**
☎ 61 13 41
Ⓤ Südbahnhof
⌚ Mon-Fri 9.30am-1pm, 2-8pm, Sat 9.30am-4pm

English-Language Newsagents
Magazines and newspapers in English and other European languages can be obtained at the newsagents near the Schillerstrasse exit at the B-Ebene level at the Hauptwache; **Süssmann's** bookshop behind the Katharinenkirche at Hauptwache; **Internationale Presse Schmidt & Hahn** at the Hauptbahnhof; and the kiosk at the corner of Siesmayerstrasse and Bockenheimer Landstrasse.

FOOD & DRINK

Aldi (2, A14)
This privately owned, no-frills operation is Germany's most successful grocery chain, and the word is spreading to the rest of Europe, most recently to Ireland and the UK. The items may be stacked in cardboard boxes, but cheapness doesn't mean compromising on quality. The fresh foods are always gone by 11am.
✉ **Berger Str 159, Bornheim** Ⓤ **Bornheim Mitte; Höhenstr**
🕘 **Mon-Fri 9am-6.30pm, Sat 9am-2pm**

Bären Treff (2, D9)
Imagine a shop entirely devoted to *Gummibären*, those most German of German bear-shaped jelly sweets! Here diabetics can join in with the special range of confection, and some of the sweets are even gelatin-free.
✉ **Schäfergasse 30**
☎ **29 19 88**
Ⓤ **Konstablerwache**
🕘 **Mon-Fri 10am-7pm, Sat 10am-4pm**

El Gusanito Mexican Shop (2, B6)
Eastern and southern European, and Asian, grocery stores are two-a-penny around town, but this little Mexican food-store is unique. Frozen guacamole and tamales, original herbs and spices, and cactus strips and chickpea flour are all imported from Mexico. Small cooked snacks are also available at lunchtime.
✉ **Eschersheimer Landstr 18, Nordend**
☎ **597 27 28**
Ⓤ **Grüneburgweg**
🕘 **Mon-Fri 10am-7pm, Sat 10am-2pm**

Fischhaus Ohrmann (2, B8) From catfish to oysters, this Nordend delicatessen sells fresh fish, cooked fish dishes and speciality wines to an appreciative clientele. The shop design is redolent of a ship, and the staff are happy to give helpful cooking tips.
✉ **Oeder Weg 71, Nordend**
☎ **59 59 98**
Ⓤ **Eschenheimer Tor**
🕘 **Mon-Fri 9am-6.30pm, Sat 8am-2pm**

Hertie (2, E9)
You may come across each of the gourmet foods and ingredients in a number of shops around Frankfurt, but not under one roof as in the basement floor at Hertie. The cheese counter is to die for, and the range of Italian pastas, balsamic vinegars and olive oils will bowl you over. It also measures up well on the Asian front.
✉ **Zeil 90** ☎ **92 90 50**
Ⓤ **Konstablerwache**
🕘 **Mon-Fri 9.30am-8pm, Sat 9am-4pm**

Krögers Markt (2, B8) The morning queue for this bakery's fresh breads stretches out to the street. That speaks for itself.
✉ **Oeder Weg 59, Nordend**
☎ **44 50 70**
Ⓤ **Eschenheimer Tor**
🕘 **Mon-Fri 7am-6.30pm, Sat 7am-2pm**

Parmesan & Worscht (2, B8) All you need for the Italian kitchen is right here: fresh pasta, olives, cheese and sausage, and also a selection of wines including some excellent Valpolicella.

Watering Holes – A Frankfurt Phenomenon

One small-business enterprise that has benefited from the restricted shopping hours is the *Trinkhalle*, also known as *Wasserhäuschen*, or watering hole. With over 350 of these kiosks dotted around the Frankfurt landscape, they're impossible to miss. Not least because there's usually a congregation of vociferous drunks and rough types with pit bulls or Dobermans hanging around outside, but their bark is usually worse than their bite! These kiosks, a unique element of Frankfurt culture since their introduction in 1868, offer a valuable service to the whole community. They're open daily 8am-11pm, and if you've forgotten the bread or milk, or some visitors have landed unexpectedly and you've got no beer in, they're life-savers. Many also stock major English-language newspapers.

Alan Benson

Care for a Kettle with your Coffee?

Don't miss out on a novel shopping opportunity at **Eduscho** or **Tchibo** coffee shops, which sell not only freshly ground coffee but also designer goods such as electrical appliances, kitchenware or even ski jackets and suits. These chains branched out beyond coffee when the coffee market went into decline some years ago. Now the non-coffee goods generate more sales than the original coffee products.

✉ Oeder Weg 66, Nordend ☎ 95 50 26 93 Ⓤ Eschenheimer Tor ⌚ Mon-Fri 9am-6.30pm, Sat 8am-2pm

Plöger (2, E6)
This Fressgasse delicatessen is a landmark on the cheese, wine and champagne front. The lunch dishes are also a major attraction, eaten standing up at high tables on the street outside.
✉ Grosse Bockenheimer Str 30 ☎ 138 71 10 Ⓤ Alte Oper; Hauptwache ⌚ Mon-Fri 9am-7pm, Sat 8.30am-4pm

WeinSocietät (1, D4)
Hidden in a yard off Leipziger Strasse, this excellent wine shop specialises in German and French wines, but it also stocks an impressive selection of Italian, Spanish and Portuguese vintages. The owner, Claus Niebuhr, is one of Germany's top 3 sommeliers and freely gives tips on flavours and choices. The 3rd Friday of every month, he offers a wine-tasting lecture at Cafe Klemm (Kiesstr 41, Bockenheim); numbers are limited.
✉ Leipziger Str 42, Bockenheim ☎ 70 56 07 Ⓤ Leipziger Str ⌚ Mon-Fri 11am-7pm, Sat 10am-4pm

Wild Horst Schmidt (2, B7) It looks like many other small-time family supermarkets until you skim through the selection of game in the refrigerator. The Schmidt family are licensed hunters, and the venison, rabbit and wild boar come from the outlying regions. The selection of heavy red wines and Graeger champagne is a perfect match.
✉ Oeder Weg 55-57, Nordend ☎ 55 66 50 Ⓤ Eschenheimer Tor ⌚ Mon-Fri 8am-7pm, Sat 8am-2pm

Martin Moos

A wine buff's treasure trove, WeinSocietät

SPECIALIST SHOPS

Beate Uhse (2, H4)
Sex toys galore from this old lady, who took her chain store to the stock market in 1999 and hasn't looked back since.
✉ **Kaiserstr 61, Bahnhofsviertel**
☎ **24 24 91 75**
Hauptbahnhof
🕒 **Mon-Fri 10am-8pm, Sat 10am-4pm**

Kool and klassy Kontrast

Biotop Naturkost & Naturkosmetik
(2, C7) This health shop does it the natural way, even down to reusable sanitary towels! Beeswax candles, natural cosmetic products and health foods are just some of the items on sale.
✉ **Oeder Weg 43, Nordend**
☎ **59 79 21 04**
Eschenheimer Tor
🕒 **Mon-Fri 9am-6.30pm, Sat 9am-1.30pm**

Euber (4, A4)
Wacky cakes made to order! Be it pig faces, giant ladybirds or musical instruments, this shop can make it and bake it.
✉ **Leipziger Str 31, Bockenheim**
☎ **77 29 52**
Leipziger Str **11**
🕒 **Mon-Fri 8.30am-6.30pm, Sat 9am-3pm, Sun 1-4pm**

Fotospezialist Martin Moog (2, E6)
Ever yearned after an original Leica, Rollei or Contax camera? This gem sells second-hand rarities and quality new photographic equipment. The Japanese may have flooded the market with mass products, but strangely this shop has a core of regular Japanese customers who keep returning to look for 'the old masters' of the photographic world. One of the few shops with 120mm Ilford film.
✉ **Kaiserhofstr 13**
☎ **13 37 94 26** **Alte Oper; Hauptwache**
🕒 **Mon-Wed 9.30am-6.30pm, Thurs-Fri 9.30am-7pm, Sat 9.30am-3pm**

Inside Her (2, D9)
Lingerie, feather boas and erotica. The shopping scene wouldn't be the same without this raunchy outlet.
✉ **Vilbeler Str 34**
☎ **29 51 00**
Konstablerwache
🕒 **Mon-Fri 12-8pm, Sat 11am-4pm**

John Montag (2, H5)
Shopping in Frankfurt wouldn't be complete without a visit to an outlet for Meissen porcelain. So do it right and visit a specialist. John Montag is one of the most reputable around.

Too cute to eat – Euber cake shop

✉ **Kaiserstr 41, Bahnhofsviertel ☎ 23 30 32 Ⓤ Willy-Brandt-Platz ⏲ Mon-Fri 9am-7pm, Sat 9am-4pm**

Kontrast (1, E11)
This designer furniture store on 6 levels is every home owner's dream. The old brick lofthouse is perfect for presenting the coveted goods that draw thousands of people from the whole region. Go on Saturday and join in the train of people moseying along to the funky background music. A real shopping experience.
✉ **Hanauer Landstr 297, Ostend ☎ 943 59 50 🚊 11, Riederhöfe ⏲ Mon-Fri 10am-7.30pm, Sat 10am-4pm**

Mercedes-Benz (2, G6) You need a big wallet to pay for the model cars and Mercedes-Benz merchandise at this shop of the branded gentry. Talk about squeezing as much mileage as possible out of a name! But actually, it's irresistible. See 3D computer graphics on the latest models, and simulate a test-drive. There's a World Coffee cafe, and a kiddies' corner.
✉ **Kaiserstr 19-21 ☎ 97 35 54 90 Ⓤ Willy-Brandt-Platz 🚊 11 ⏲ Mon-Fri 10am-7.30pm, Sat 10am-4pm**

Sabine Seus (2, C3)
This interior design specialist is in good company with 58's Buy Heidt designer clothing outlet across the road. Sabine Seus does it with amazing lamps and household goods.
✉ **Kronberger Str 22, Westend ☎ 97 20 65 22 Ⓤ Westend ⏲ Mon-Fri 11am-7pm, Sat 11am-4pm**

Steinway & Sons (2, B8) The Ferrari of grand pianos. Steinway originally came from the Harz region of northern Germany. This outlet holds occasional concerts so audiences can hear for themselves the tone quality that has ensured this company's success.
✉ **Oeder Weg 59, Nordend ☎ 59 79 10 06 Ⓤ Eschenheimer Tor ⏲ Mon-Fri 10am-6.30pm, Sat 10am-2pm**

Tabak Fischer (2, H4)
This tobacconist has the quality of an old curiosity shop, which makes it a favourite address for John Aylesbury and Havana fans.
✉ **Münchener Str 22, Bahnhofsviertel ☎ 23 58 85 Ⓤ Hauptbahnhof 🚊 11 ⏲ Mon-Fri 9am-6pm**

Martin Moos

The grandest of grand pianos, Steinway & Sons

places to eat

For a city its size, Frankfurt is remarkably sophisticated in the gastronomy stakes. Not surprising then that dining out is a favoured pastime. It's also extremely good value compared with, say, Paris or London. And the selection is so broad, it's possible to sample a different restaurant every night for a whole year and still be nowhere near where you started.

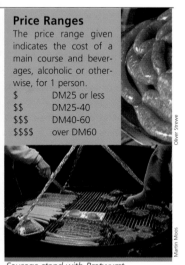

Price Ranges

The price range given indicates the cost of a main course and beverages, alcoholic or otherwise, for 1 person.

$	DM25 or less
$$	DM25-40
$$$	DM40-60
$$$$	over DM60

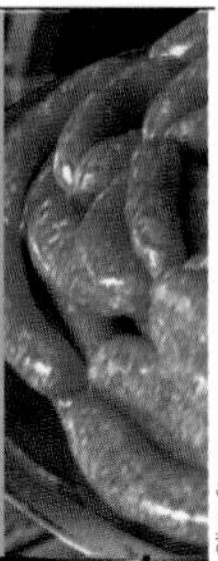

Oliver Strewe

Martin Moos

Sausage stand with Bratwurst

Local fare is heavy, to say the least, and if you were half-hearted about meat before, there's a good chance you'll be put off pork and beef for life. But don't despair. New German cuisine has blown a fresh wind through the Frankfurt kitchen (no pun intended for those who've already had the pleasure of sampling the local speciality, 'hand-cheese').

There's also a heavy Mediterranean slant among Frankfurt restaurants. High-quality Italian restaurants are abundant, and swank French and Iberian eateries are as easy to find as Greek and Turkish delights.

The upsurge in Asian restaurants is rapidly changing the gastronomic landscape. A growing Japanese population has spurred on the arrival of the sushi brigade, though the quality varies. Good Thai and Indian food is also par for the course.

Frankfurt's outdoor restaurants are probably the city's best gastronomic draw card. Brunch is a popular weekend pastime, and most restaurants serve throughout the day, usually until 11pm or later.

Local Delicacies

Sauerkraut with *Kassler*, or boiled ham, is a big seller, as is the slab of pork shoulder served with purée called *Schäufelchen* (the 'shovel' of the name is the bone on which the meat is served). *Haspel*, the boiled leg of pork, is not for the faint-hearted, as the tools supplied reveal. A lighter offering is the *Grüne Sosse*, a delicious cold sauce essentially made from yogurt, 7 spring herbs, onion and garlic and served with potatoes and boiled eggs, or ox meat.

Paying Up

It's usual for groups to settle their bill individually, and waiters will take the time to calculate for each person. Service is included, but an additional 5-10% tip is standard. Beware: credit cards aren't a trusted form of payment, with Eurocard or Visa more frequently accepted than American Express. Many Frankfurt eateries will only accept cash.

Frankfurt is the birthplace of the *Frankfurter*, also known as the *Wiener* or hot dog in other parts of the world. Only meat producers licensed to grade their sausages as *Original Frankfurter Würstchen* can market their goods as such, but amazingly the only licensed producers of the Frankfurter are located in the nearby town of Neu-Isenburg!

Handkäse mit Musik is a local snack that has been the downfall of many a poor tourist: doused with vinegar, oil, raw onions and caraway seeds, this rather pungent 'hand-cheese' takes some getting used to. A more biddable sort of cheese is the *Schneegestöber*, whipped camembert with onions and paprika powder.

Dining Districts

Fressgasse, nearby Opernplatz and the streets behind the Katharinenkirche at the Hauptwache, are key restaurant areas.

In Bornheim, Upper and Lower Berger Strasse buzz with outdoor cafes and bistros, and Sandweg offers some multicultural delights. Linking Bornheim and Nordend, the Alleenring is dotted with a number of good eateries, as are Oeder Weg, Rotlintstrasse, Friedberger Landstrasse and Glauburgstrasse (but these are more spread out).

Liebigstrasse and Grüneburgweg are key Westend locations, while Konrad-Brosswitz-Strasse and Leipziger Strasse are Bockenheim's magnets.

In Sachsenhausen, Schweizer Strasse and Alt-Sachsenhausen offer chic bistros and applewine taverns.

Midday Rush Hour

Frankfurters aren't hurried folk, but they like to rush their midday food – which is why fast-food diners are two-a-penny. Sausage stands and the traditional bakery with *belegte Brötchen* (stuffed bread rolls) still rule the roost.

Don't leave Frankfurt without trying the spice-bomb Currywurst at the **Snack Point** sausage stand (2, B5; ☎ 72 11 29), Grüneburgweg 37, Westend. Try its Jambalaya Wurst too, or perhaps another local institution, potato cakes with apple mousse.

The trendy sandwich bar idea is catching on here. Try the **Energy Eatery** (2, G5; ☎ 23 80 27 33), Kaiserstr 38; the **Brezel Company** (4, A4; ☎ 0180-555 62 22), Leipziger Str 1; and **Sandwicher** (2, B4; ☎ 71 03 40 67), Reuterweg 63 and (☎ 74 30 90 84) Westendstr 27 (2, F2).

Martin Moos

Lunch on the run

BAHNHOFSVIERTEL

Ginger (2, J4) **$$**
Bistro
The sleek Asian decor gives away the gastronomic accent at this elusive bistro. Try the dim sum platter or Sichuan duck. The sushi is acceptable and there's a selection of European dishes. Bookings advisable. Good for business lunches.
✉ **Windmühlstr 14 ☎ 23 17 71 Ⓜ Hauptbahnhof; Willy-Brandt-Platz 🚊 11 ⏲ 10.30am-midnight ♿ V**

Indian Curry House (2, H4) **$**
Indian
The location may not be the most appetising, but you'll forget this once you tuck into the chicken curry or the vegetable samosas. Bookings essential (evenings). Accepts all credit cards.
✉ **Weserstr 17 ☎ 23 59 86 Ⓜ Hauptbahnhof; Willy-Brand-Platz 🚊 11 ⏲ 11am-11pm (Sun from 1pm) ♿ V**

Kabuki (2, G5) **$$$**
Japanese
Bring a few friends and be entertained by a sumo wrestler deftly cooking up a storm on the teppan grill before you. The expensive 5-course Yokozuna or Ohseki menus look daunting, but have expertly judged portions. Lunch menus are cheaper and include noodle soup and dessert. Smart dress. Bookings advisable.
✉ **Kaiserstr 42 ☎ 23 43 53 Ⓜ Willy-Brandt-Platz 🚊 11 ⏲ Mon-Fri 12-2pm, Mon-Sat 6pm-midnight ♿ V**

Rainbow Garden (2, H2) **$$**
Thai
One of Frankfurt's best Thai houses, just a stone's throw from the trade fairs. The food turns up at conveyer-belt speed, but the tempo doesn't compromise the quality. Lunch specials and a wide range of fowl and seafood. Don't miss Sunday brunch, all you can eat for DM30/16; beverages extra. Bookings essential. Accepts all credit cards.
✉ **Düsseldorfer Str 1-7 ☎ 25 20 66 Ⓜ Hauptbahnhof ⏲ 11.30am-2.30pm, 5.30-11.30pm ♿ V**

Tse Yang (2, H3) **$$**
Chinese
While good Asian eateries are two-a-penny in Frankfurt, you'll be hard pushed to find a quality Chinese. This is one of the few whose dishes don't taste as though they've all come out of the same pot. Bookings advisable.
✉ **Kaiserstr 67 ☎ 23 25 41 Ⓜ Hauptbahnhof ⏲ 11.30am-11.30pm ♿ V**

Frankfurt's Best Beer Gardens

No-one, but no-one, wants to sit indoors on a hot summer's evening. The following are the best beer gardens around:

Gerbermühle (1, G10; ☎ 965 22 90), Deutschherrnufer 105, Sachsenhausen

Zur Sonne (1, C10; ☎ 45 93 96), Berger Str 312, Bornheim

Zum Rad (1, A11; ☎ 47 91 28), Leonhardsgasse 2, Seckbach

Zur Stalburg (1, D7; ☎ 55 79 34), Glauburgstr 80, Nordend

Friedberger Warte (1, B8; ☎ 59 24 65), Friedberger Landstr 360, Nordend

Dauth Schneider (2, J10; ☎ 61 35 33), Klappergasse 39, Sachsenhausen

Schreiber Heyne (1, H8; ☎ 62 39 63), Mörfelder Landstr 11, Sachsenhausen

Wäldches (1, A3; ☎ 52 05 22), Am Ginnheimer Wäldchen 8, Ginnheim

BOCKENHEIM

Abendmahl (1, D3) $
International
The name means Last Supper, but that's the only religious overtone. Still, thinking about it, some of the tables could seat 13. A tiny living room with couch and armchairs is perfect for lounging after one of the wholesome meals from this excellent student diner. Bookings advisable.
✉ **Florastr 24 ☎ 70 25 55 Ⓤ Kirchplatz ⌚ 6pm-1am (Sun from 10am) ♿ V**

Al Arischa (1, D3) $$
African/Middle Eastern
Lebanese restaurants are beginning to make their mark in town. Here, you may not need to look further than the long list of starters (over 50 at last count), which can easily be combined to form a mixed platter. Bookings advisable.
✉ **Leipziger Str 108 ☎ 77 22 57 Ⓤ Leipziger Str; Kirchplatz ⌚ Mon-Sat 6pm-midnight, Sun only during trade fairs ♿ V**

Albatross (4, B4) $
Cafe
Students will eat anything, but they're spoiled for choice at this hotspot. Brunch just wouldn't be the same without its redoubtable muesli. Cheese and sausage platters come with wholegrain bread rolls and croissants. And I'll bet it's the only place in town to serve Ovomaltine.
✉ **Kiesstr 27 ☎ 707 27 69 Ⓤ Bockenheimer Warte 🚌 32, 33, 50 ⌚ 9am-midnight (Sat-Sun to 8pm) ♿ V**

Chew & View

Some great spots for dining while enjoying sweeping views:

Henninger Turm, Sachsenhausen (p. 81)
Lohrberg Schänke, Seckbach (p. 85)
Main Tower Bar & Restaurant (p. 77)
Windows 25 (p. 78)

Andalucia (1, D3) $$
Spanish
The residents of Konrad-Brosswitz-Strasse are spoilt for choice with its nest of cosy eateries. Andalucia has a tantalising array of tapas including garlic mushrooms and salty fried sardines. If rabbit or lamb don't tickle your tonsils, the fried baby squid or mixed fish platter are interesting alternatives to the standard paella. Bookings essential.
✉ **Konrad-Brosswitz-Str 41 ☎ 77 37 30 Ⓤ Kirchplatz ⌚ 6pm-1am ♿**

Champions (4, C4) $$$
American
This American sports bar is quarterback size and seats over 200. It does the usual Tex-Mex fare yards better than anywhere else in Frankfurt. Dinner reservations up to 7pm only. Accepts all credit cards.
✉ **Marriott Hotel, Hamburger Allee 2-10, Bockenheim/Westend ☎ 77 33 00 Ⓤ Bockenheimer Warte 🚋 16, 19 ⌚ noon-2am ♿**

Coffee Breaks

Many Frankfurters don't like to sit down over a coffee, so you will see lots of coffee shops simply with a few high tables to lean your elbows on while you slurp. **World Coffee** on Börsenstrasse (2, E6) and Grüneburgweg (1, E6), **Lavazza** on Gr Bockenheimer Strasse (2, E5) and Zeilgalerie (2, E8), and **Nescafe** on Kleine Bockenheimer Strasse (2, E6) are busy spots with excellent coffee.

Oliver Strewe

BORNHEIM

Cafe Wacker
(2, A15) **$**
Cafe
Wake up and smell the coffee! The younger sister of the original Cafe Wacker at Kornmarkt, this coffee shop housed in a protected building feels like it's been around for years. The many roast blends are freshly ground on site. High ceilings and a polished wood finish complete the picture.
✉ Berger Str 185 ☎ 46 00 77 52 Ⓤ Bornheim Mitte 🚊 12 🕘 Mon-Sat 8am-7pm, Sun 9am-6pm

Calabrese (2, A15) **$$**
Italian
Forget Rome, it's right here. The pizzas at Calabrese are better than you'll get anywhere else this side of the Dolomites. Its simple charm is a nice change from some of the more sterile Italian places around. But don't tell a soul; gems like this are best kept a secret. Bookings advisable. Takes AmEx, Visa or Eurocard.
✉ Arnsburger Str 70 ☎ 43 46 68 Ⓤ Bornheim Mitte 🚊 12 🕘 Sun-Fri 11am-3pm, 6-10pm, Sat 8-10.30pm V

Hannibal
(2, A15) **$$/$$$**
Bistro
The downstairs bistro is better value and more lively than the elegant 1st-floor restaurant, which is over-priced and has a limited menu but attentive service and tasteful surrounds compensate. Two's company, three's a crowd. Smart dress. Bookings advisable. No credit cards.
✉ Berger Str 185-187 ☎ 94 50 04 44 Ⓤ Bornheim Mitte 🚊 12 🕘 10-1am (Sat to 2am)

El Pacifico
(2, C12) **$/$$**
Mexican
This popular young hangout gets 10 out of 10 for atmosphere. OK, the food's fake Mexican, but it's not bad by any means. The nachos con rajas pack a good punch, as do the spicy chicken wings and the stuffed jalapenos. But the standard burritos, tostadas, tacos and fajitas are on the bland side. Bookings essential. No credit cards.
✉ Sandweg 79, Bornheim/Nordend ☎ 44 69 88 Ⓤ Merianplatz 🕘 5pm-midnight V

Indefinite (2, C13) **$**
Cafe
This tiny New Age hangout democratically allows guests to only sit for a maximum 1½hrs, about enough time to dig into the DM15 all-you-can-eat weekend brunch and a freshly squeezed fruit juice. There are also free coffee refills, rare in Frankfurt. Bookings essential on weekends.
✉ Sandweg 64, Bornheim/Nordend ☎ 43 50 55 Ⓤ Merianplatz 🕘 Tues-Sat 10am-10pm, Sun 10am-7pm V

Koh Samui
(1, D10) **$$$**
Thai
If there was a rule that said the less ornate a Thai restaurant is, the better the food tastes, then this one would fit the bill perfectly. It's tiny and it's basic, but it's famous for its kitchen. Bookings advisable.
✉ Berger Str 252 ☎ 46 15 94 Ⓤ Bornheim Mitte 🚊 12 🕘 11.30am-3pm, 5.30pm-midnight V

Manolya (2, B13) **$**
Turkish
It's loud, family-friendly, and the best Turkish restaurant in town. What more can I say? Oh yeah, the ginormous menu means you have to return again and again to sample more of the 50-odd dishes on offer. And it's a vegetarian haven. Bookings essential.
✉ Habsburgerallee 6a ☎ 494 01 62 Ⓤ Höhenstr 🕘 6pm-1am (Fri-Sat to 2am) V

Suvadee (2, D11) **$$**
Thai
Ask anyone what's the best Thai address in town, and

One of the district's bohemian eateries

they'll say Suvadee. But do they mean the one in the Steinweg-Passage, or in Baumweg? Well, they're sisters, so it doesn't matter. This one is more off the beaten track, so it feels more exclusive. Bookings essential.
✉ Baumweg 19, Bornheim/Nordend ☎ 494 07 64 Ⓤ Merianplatz ⏲ Mon-Fri 12-3pm, 6-11pm, Sat 12-11pm ♿ V

Weisse Lilie (1, D10) $$
Spanish
Only half the tables can be reserved at this Bornheim institution, allowing a steady flow of drop-in diners. Don't be shy about joining a table with a free seat. It may be your only chance to sample the mouth-watering shrimps or the lamb ragout. Pass on the tortilla. Bookings advisable. Credit cards unenthusiastically accepted.
✉ Berger Str 275 ☎ 45 38 60 Ⓤ Bornheim Mitte 🚋 12 ⏲ 5pm-2am ♿

Food for Thought

The only English-language guide to dining out in Frankfurt is the *MainCity Food & Drink Guide* (DM14.80), available at larger newsagents and foreign-language bookshops. German-language guides include the annually updated *Frankfurt Geht Aus!* (DM8.80), put out by the weekly magazine *Journal Frankfurt*. A handier book to carry around is the *Stadtbuch Frankfurt* (DM18.90), a complete guide to Frankfurt including a good dining out section.

CENTRE

Altes Cafe Schneider (2, G6) $
Cafe
One of Frankfurt's oldest family-run enterprises. The city just wouldn't be the same without this traditional coffee house.
✉ Kaiserstr 12 ☎ 28 14 47 Ⓤ Hauptwache; Willy-Brandt-Platz ⏲ Mon-Fri 7am-7pm, Sat 8am-6pm, Sun 12-6pm winter only ♿

Avocado (2, D6) **$$$**
Bistro
A place that's led the growing tide of gourmet bistros, Avocado is the best in its class. Bookings are essential. Accepts all credit cards except Diners.
✉ Hochstr 27 ☎ 29 28 67 Ⓤ Hauptwache; Alte Oper ⏲ Mon-Sat 12-2.30pm, 6-10.30pm ♿ V

Bistro Merhaba (2, E7) $
Turkish
The crowds haven't stopped pouring in since this Turkish takeaway opened in 1999. Most are after a crispy döner or the best falafel sandwich in town. Eat in or take out, but cancel that dentist's appointment for the garlic might anaesthetize them.
✉ An der Hauptwache, Hauptwache Passage 45, B-Ebene ☎ 13 37 68 64 Ⓤ Hauptwache ⏲ Mon-Fri 9.30am-8pm, Sat 10am-4pm ♿ V

Brasserie an der Alten Oper (2, E5) $$
French
The location alone is a winner for this prominent brasserie at the edge of Opernplatz, not to mention the masterful French cuisine. The tables outside are prized possessions. Ask the waiter to recommend a dish from the changing daily menu. Fish is a speciality, and the salads are exquisite. Bookings are

Business Restaurants

If you want to do your deals over lunch or dinner, try these places:

City Centre Brasserie an der Alten Oper (p. 75), Higematsu, Mutter Ernst, Oscar's, Plaza, Ristorante Garibaldi, Sushi Circle (all p. 77), Utage (p. 78)

Westend Bettina-Eck (p. 83), Gargantua (p. 83), Morton's Steakhouse, Ristorante Isoletta, Stars & Starlet, Surf 'n' Turf (all p. 84)

Bahnhofsviertel Ginger, Kabuki, Rainbow Garden (all p. 72)

Cultural cuisine at the Alte Oper cafe

essential. Accepts Visa or Eurocard.
✉ **Opernplatz 8**
☎ **91 39 86 34** Ⓜ **Alte Oper** ⓘ **11-1am** ♿ **V**

Cafe Metropol (3, C4) **$**
Cafe
You'll forgive the forgetful staff anything at this bright, central meeting point. The early bird gets the seat outside on the garden terrace under the clang of the cathedral bells. You won't manage to finish the massive brunch offerings, never mind the gigantic milk coffees. The cup it overfloweth!
✉ **Weckmarkt 13-15**
☎ **28 82 87** Ⓜ **Römer** ⓘ **Tues-Fri 9-1am, Sat-Sun 9-2am** ♿ **V**

Da Scalpi (2, E5) **$**
Italian
If there was a world speed record for pizza-making, this place would hold it. And the former trading floor at the Frankfurt bourse wouldn't hold a candle to the noise. A hot tip: pizza salami with pepperoni. The spaghetti vongole or the lasagne with gorgonzola aren't bad also.
✉ **Hochstr 51** ☎ **28 22 26** Ⓜ **Alte Oper** ⓘ **Mon-Fri 10.30am-8pm, Sat 10.30am-4pm** **V**

Die Leiter (2, E6) **$$**
Bistro
Modern Mediterranean is the order of the day at this swank bistro off the Fressgasse that swarms with bankers at lunch-time and attracts a chic clientele in the evenings. Excellent dining at matching prices, and a wine list to die for. Smart dress. Bookings essential.
✉ **Kaiserhofstr 11**
☎ **29 21 21**
Ⓜ **Hauptwache; Alte Oper** ⓘ **Mon-Sat 12-3pm, 6-11pm** ♿ **V**

Eckstein (3, A5) **$$$**
Bistro
Gourmet delights under the remains of the old inner city walls. Despite its hidden location, chances are you won't get a table; book in advance. The summer garden is Frankfurt's best. Smart dress. Accepts all credit cards.
✉ **An der Staufenmauer 7** ☎ **131 07 27**
Ⓜ **Konstablerwache**
ⓘ **Mon-Fri 12-2.30pm, Mon-Sat 6-10.30pm** **V**

Exedra (2, E10) **$$$**
Greek
Situated opposite the law chambers, this upmarket establishment holds its own court as the master of all Greek restaurants. This is modern Greek cuisine at its best; it lacks the warmth of a taverna, though. Bookings advisable. Accepts all credit cards.
✉ **Heiligkreuzgasse 29**
☎ **28 73 97** Ⓜ **Konstablerwache** 🚊 **12**
ⓘ **Mon-Thurs 8.30-1am, Fri-Sat 8-2am, Sun 4pm-1am** ♿ **V**

Fisch Franke (3, B3) **$**
Seafood
Tourists manage to find their way here without the help of guidebooks, but it's still worth mentioning as a great tip for fresh fish at low prices. French fries and fried potatoes are the usual accomplices.
✉ **Domstr 9-11**
☎ **29 62 61** Ⓜ **Römer**
🚊 **11** ⓘ **Mon-Fri 10.30am-8.30pm, Sat 10.30am-4pm** ♿

Higematsu (2, E6) **$$**
Japanese
One of the better sushi addresses in town, Higematsu also does some mean udon and soba soups. The high percentage of Japanese guests speaks for its authenticity. Bookings advisable. Accepts all credit cards.
✉ Meisengasse 11 ☎ 28 06 88 Ⓤ Hauptwache ⌚ Mon-Sat 12.30-2.30pm, Mon-Fri 6.30-10.30pm, Sat 6-10pm ♿ V

Iwase (2, D9) **$$$**
Japanese
With just 4 small tables and a few stools at the counter, this sushi bar is in high demand. Once a real insider tip, now it's the worst-kept secret in town. Try a multicourse fixed menu for a true appreciation of the chef's expertise. At peak times it's impossible to get a seat. Bookings essential.
✉ Vilbeler Str 31 ☎ 28 39 92 Ⓤ Konstablerwache ⌚ Tues-Sat 12-2pm, Tues-Sun 6.30-10pm ♿ V

Main Tower Bar & Restaurant (2, F5) **$$**
International
See it and weep! This is a rare opportunity to view Frankfurt from the vantage of a high-rise. Alas, in March 2000 the restaurant was already booked out up to November. Who cares whether the food is good, or if each drink costs a few marks extra. You wouldn't even begrudge the DM6 elevator fee. Thankfully, a public viewing gallery opened in April 2000. Smart dress.
✉ Neue Mainzer Str 52-58 ☎ 36 50 47 70 Ⓤ Willy-Brandt-Platz; Alte Oper; Taunusanlage ⌚ 10-1am (Fri-Sat to 2am) ♿ V

Mutter Ernst (2, F6) **$$**
Traditional Frankfurt
No-nonsense home-cooking with a limited choice. From top-level bankers down to students, you have to eat what's put in front of you at this Frankfurt institution. Go Friday for a liquid lunch; Saturday is locals' day out. No credit cards accepted.
✉ Alte Rothofstr 12 ☎ 28 38 22 Ⓤ Hauptwache; Taunusanlage; Alte Oper ⌚ Mon-Fri 9am-midnight, Sat 9.30am-5pm ♿

Oscar's (2, G6) **$$**
Italian
See-and-be-seen doing business over a dish of gnocchi gorgonzola or a plate of grilled salmon. The quality of the food served doesn't quite match the prices, but it doesn't stop the steady lunch-time flow. Bookings are essential. Smart dress. Accepts Visa or Eurocard.
✉ Am Kaiserplatz ☎ 21 51 50 Ⓤ Willy-Brandt-Platz ⌚ 11-1am ♿ V

Paninoteca (3, A1) **$$**
Italian
This city-centre Italian does a roaring lunch-time trade, and service runs like clockwork. But try an evening meal for real personality. The gnocchi gorgonzola or the rucola salad come up trumps every time. Bookings essential. Smart dress. No credit cards.
✉ Bleidenstr 12 ☎ 28 44 87 Ⓤ Hauptwache ⌚ Mon-Sat 11-1am, closed Sun ♿ V

Plaza (2, G6) **$**
Food hall
Swim with the sea of suits that descends at noon on the ground floor of the Commerzbank building, Frankfurt's largest public canteen. You can compile your own salad, or sample the freshly prepared Asian selections. But there's a danger your lunch could be cold by the time you find a seat.
✉ Am Kaiserplatz Ⓤ Willy-Brandt-Platz ⌚ Mon-Fri 11.30am-5pm, Sun 11am-2pm V

Ristorante Garibaldi (2, E6) **$$**
Italian
The chef himself mingles with guests, taking orders and making recommendations. Heed him when he points to the salmon carpaccio. Try the vegetable antipasti selection, or torture yourself choosing between the endless range of pasta dishes. Bookings advisable. Accepts Visa or Eurocard.
✉ Klein Hochstr 4 ☎ 21 99 76 44 Ⓤ Hauptwache; Alte Oper ⌚ Mon-Sat 11am-11.30pm, Sun only during trade fairs ♿ V

Sushi Circle (2, E5) **$$**
Japanese
Sushi on a conveyer belt. This popular novelty lunch-time spot may not have the best sushi in town, but it's commendable at these low prices. Miso soup and nigiri sushi do the rounds.

Takeaway lunch boxes are available. Accepts AmEx, Visa, Eurocard or Diners.
✉ **Neue Mainzer Str 84**
☎ **91 39 93 02**
Alte Oper, Taunusanlage ⏲ **12-11pm**
V

Utage (2, G5) **$$$**
Japanese
Choose from 3 rooms: the sushi bar, the teppan grill room or the main lobby, which serves everything from noodle dishes to the full kaiseki. Utage is in the premier league of Japanese restaurants in Frankfurt, and it's popular with Japanese guests. Bookings essential. Smart dress. Accepts AmEx, Visa, Eurocard or Diners.
✉ **Taunustor 2** ☎ **25 38 26** **Hauptwache; Taunusanlage; Willy-Brandt-Platz** ⏲ **Mon-Sat 12-2.30pm, 6-10pm** **V**

Windows 25
(2, G5) **$**
Food Hall
A seat in this upmarket food hall on the 25th floor of the Japan Center is a prized possession. The above-average canteen food includes an antipasti buffet and freshly prepared stir-fry combinations; pay by weight.
✉ **Taunustor 2**
☎ **27 40 41 48**
Hauptwache; Willy-Brandt-Platz; Taunusanlage ⏲ **Mon-Fri 11.30am-2.30pm, Thurs 5-8pm, Sun 11am-3pm**
V

Late-Night Eats

Some unbeatable late-night eateries include:

Asian Bar (2, D6; ☎ 133 80 00), Hilton Hotel, Hochstr 4 – serves till 4am

Central Park (2, E6; ☎ 91 39 61 46), Kaiserhofstr 12 – serves a blend of modern Mediterranean and Asian on Friday and Saturday till 2am

Helium (3, A1; ☎ 28 70 35), Bleidenstr 7 – a trendy bar with a small but impressive night-time menu served till 3am

Jimmy's, Hotel Hessischer Hof, Friedrich-Ebert-Anlage 40 (2, G1) – dishes up German specialities, modern European food and thick cigars till 3am

Kontiki (2, D7; ☎ 29 66 50), Grosse Eschenheimer Str 20 – a Thai restaurant also open to 4am

Maximilian (2, J7; ☎ 61 71 46), Schweizer Str 1 – a smart Sachsenhausen bistro serving quality food until 3am

Shooters (3, B3; ☎ 28 28 38), Domstr 4 – an Australian pub and diner preparing not-half-bad burgers and pancakes till 4am

Tigerpalast (2, E10; ☎ 92 00 22 25), Heiligkreuzgasse 16-20 – the elegant gourmet restaurant in the cellar of the Tigerpalast vaudeville theatre (p. 98) boasts a Michelin star and serves dinner until 1am Tues-Sun

NORDEND

Cafe Kante
(2, C12) **$**
Cafe
It's hard to find a better spot to while away a few hours writing postcards than this coffeeshop/bakery. Try the tiny cheesecakes, or indeed any of the sweet offerings made on the premises. The garden makes the day.
✉ **Kantstr 13** ☎ **499 00 83** **Merianplatz** ⏲ **7am-8pm (Sun from 10am)**

Cafe Wacker (2, B7) **$**
Cafe
A hit among locals for its huge brunch platters and generous slices of cake. Service can be 'iffy' when the place is teeming, usually Saturday and Sunday around noon. But this doesn't detract from the comfortable seating, idyllic back garden and overall comeliness of the place.
✉ **Mittelweg 47** ☎ **55 02 42** **Musterschule; Eschenheimer Tor**
36 ⏲ **Mon-Fri 8am-7pm, Sat 8am-6pm, Sun 9am-6pm** **V**

Deux Lions
(1, C7) **$$$**
Vegetarian
If they wait a few years, the decor might have com-

pleted the full circle and be fashionable again. The pancakes decked with juicy vegetables and melted cheese hit the nail square on the head, though. Bookings advisable.
✉ Adickesallee 51-53 ☎ 59 79 08 91 Miquel-/Adickesallee ⌚ Mon-Fri 11.30am-2.30pm, 6-10.30pm V

Eckhaus (2, B12) **$**
International
It's the potato röstis that have guests scrambling to get in the door. Try them with a yogurt dressing, or topped with Swiss raclette cheese, or ham and mozzarella. Creative soups, scrumptious salads and excellent Schnitzel make this one of Frankfurt's most popular hideouts. Bookings advisable.
✉ Bornheimer Landstr 45 ☎ 49 11 97 Merianplatz 30 ⌚ 6pm-1am V

Exil (2, B10) **$$$**
Bistro
An inventive Euro-Asian kitchen has made this a valuable Nordend tip. The decor artfully blends old and new, reflecting the management style. It attracts a colourful clientele. The elevated prices make it a choice for a special occasion. Bookings advisable. Accepts Visa only.
✉ Mercatorstr 26 ☎ 44 72 00 Musterschule 30 ⌚ 6pm-1am (Fri-Sat to 2am) V

Gaststätte Rink (2, B13) **$**
Traditional Frankfurt
It's fondly known as 'Oma Rink' after the old woman who once ran this ancient establishment tucked away down a small alley off Musikantenweg. People come in droves for the garden in summer, and to play cards in winter. And, of course, the food.
✉ Musikantenweg 68 ☎ 43 26 59 Merianplatz ⌚ 5pm-1am (Fri-Sat to 2am)

Grössenwahn (1, D8) **$**
International
Its original cuisine and camp atmosphere have long made Grössenwahn a major crowd-puller, gay and mixed. It's impossible to feel alone in this high-spirited restaurant/meeting place. And the menu's full of surprises. Bookings advisable.
✉ Lenaustr 97 (cnr Schwarzburgstr) ☎ 59 93 56 Glauburgstr ⌚ 4pm-2am (Fri-Sat to 3am) V

Knossos (2, B12) **$$**
Greek
But for the name, you could mistake this place for a chic Italian, until you glance through the generous menu from feta and grilled zucchini starters to deep-fried squid and lamb. It's a tad over-priced, though. Bookings advisable. Accepts all credit cards.
✉ Luisenstr 7 ☎ 44 47 96 Merianplatz ⌚ 11.30-2am (Fri-Sat to 3am) V

La Trattoria (2, A5) **$$$**
Italian
Its charming rustic decor sets this Italian apart from its peers, and belies its exclusive offerings. Sit for hours over the 4-course or 7-course house specials, or go for the imaginative variations of traditional dishes. Bookings essential.
✉ Fürstenbergerstr 179 ☎ 55 21 30 Holzhausenstr 36 ⌚ Mon-Fri 12-2.30pm, 6-10pm, Sat & Sun only during trade fairs V

Las Tapas (2, B11) **$**
Spanish
Don't be surprised if some guests burst into a flamenco at this family-run establishment; chances are they'll be high-spirited relatives enjoying a night out. Good simple fare in basic surrounds, with the best tortilla in town, garlic shrimps to die for and Rioja from the keg. Bookings advisable on weekends.
✉ Friedberger Landstr 62 ☎ 43 83 05 Musterschule 30 ⌚ 5.30pm-2am

Naturbar (2, B7) **$**
Vegetarian
You need go no further than the avocado and cheese-filled pita bread. Lunch-times are crowded, so maybe an evening visit is better to sample the full gauntlet of this kitchen (bookings advisable).
✉ Oeder Weg 26 ☎ 55 44 86

Vegetarian Victuals

If you're not into eating flesh, you might find Frankfurt cuisine a challenge. For a good vegetarian meal, try **Deux Lions**, **Naturbar** or **Wolkenbruch**, all in Nordend.

Eschenheimer Tor Mon-Sat 11.30am-3.30pm, 6-11pm V

Omonia (1, D6) $
Greek
This neighbourhood Greek taverna, a favourite with locals, doesn't shy on the helpings. Bookings advisable. No credit cards.
Vogtstr 43 ☎ 59 33 14 Holzhausenstr Mon-Fri 12-2.30pm, daily 6pm-1am

Quan Van (1, D8) $
Vietnamese
This is the most popular of the 3 Quan Van restaurants in town (the others are in Hainerweg, Sachsenhausen, and Schlossstrasse, Bockenheim). You won't be disappointed with the choice, though the meals themselves are pretty standard. Bookings advisable.
Schwarzburgstr 7 ☎ 59 97 23 Glauburgstr Mon-Fri 12-3pm, daily 6pm-midnight V

Strandcafe (2, B9) $
Moroccan/Cafe
This airy cafe on 2 levels has become one of Frankfurt's best insider tips for a weekend brunch, continental and North African-style. It also has a wonderful array of salads, soups, snacks and traditional Moroccan dishes. The hummus and aubergine mousse are exquisite. Bookings advisable.
Koselstr 46 ☎ 55 72 24 Musterschule Mon-Sat 9am-10pm V

Wolkenbruch (1, D8) $
Vegetarian
This place has real flair with its 20 pizzas, ambitious salads and luxurious cheeses, and is arguably the best in the vegetarian stakes. No smoking is allowed Sunday and Monday.
Rotlintstr 47 ☎ 43 18 59 Glauburgstr Mon-Sat 6-11pm, Sun 5-10pm V

Zur Schoenen Muellerin (2, D12) $$
Traditional Frankfurt
One of Frankfurt's oldest and most colourful taverns. It's not unusual to see gay couples accompanied by their grannies here, and the staff's blue embroidered shirts add even more colour. The Schnitzel and the Frankfurter Grüne Sosse are unbeatable (not so the cheese-filled potato croquettes). Bookings advisable. Accepts AmEx, Visa or Eurocard, no Diners.
Baumweg 12 ☎ 43 20 69 Merianplatz 4pm-midnight

OSTEND

Abessinia (2, E12) $$
African/Middle Eastern
Ethiopians and Eritreans are at home at this lively restaurant, where the food thankfully hasn't been toned down for the European palate. And, in true fashion, it's hands only. Bright African paintings and table drawings are an optical extra. Bookings advisable.
Pfingsweidstr 2 ☎ 43 91 08 Zoo 6-11.30pm V

Martin Moos

Bloomin' good food

Rosengarten (1, E11) $$
International
These former Nordend restaurant owners are now experimenting in Frankfurt's 'Wild East'. The decor in this old brewery house is warm and perfectly kitschy. The kitchen adds flamboyance to the solid, southern European fare. Bookings advisable.
Hanauer Landstr 198 ☎ 94 41 38 23 11, Schwedlerstr Mon-Fri 11.30am-2.30pm, 6pm-1am, Sat 6pm-midnight V

Tao (2, D11) $$
Vietnamese
The choice is agonizingly good at Tao, regarded as the top Vietnamese venue in Frankfurt. The Quan Van threesome in Bockenheim, Nordend and Sachsenhausen are the only serious contenders, but it's Tao's roast duck that tips the balance. Bookings advisable.
Friedberger Anlage 14 ☎ 44 98 44 Zoo Tues-Fri, Sun 12-2.30pm, Tues-Sun 6-11pm V

SACHSENHAUSEN

Bodega Los Gitanos (2, J10) $$$
Spanish
Tapas and paella are the signatures, while dishes such as the special fish platter starter are adventurous. The enchiladas may even be better than at any Mexican restaurants around. The whitewashed walls and pictures of matadors and flamenco dancers add to the authentic ambience. Bookings advisable. Accepts Eurocard.
✉ **Paradiesgasse 21**
☎ **62 37 63** Ⓤ **Lokalbahnhof** 🚌 **33**
🕘 **Tues-Sun 6pm-2am** 👶

Die Gans (2, K7) **$$**
Bistro
The innovative kitchen at Die Gans ('the goose') transforms even a mundane breakfast into a dining experience. But don't limit yourself to mornings to sample the creative concoctions of this superb bistro, a new addition to the Sachsenhausen gastronomic scene. Bookings advisable at weekends. Accepts all credit cards except Diners.
✉ **Schweizer Str 76**
☎ **61 50 75**
Ⓤ **Schweizer Platz**
🕘 **11-1am** 👶 **V**

Fichtekränzi (2, J10) $
Traditional Frankfurt
Choose between local dishes and countrywide seasonal offerings, including fresh asparagus around June. The food may not quite match the high standards of other taverns, but Fichtekränzi is worth recommending for its warm atmosphere and friendly staff. Bookings advisable. No credit cards.
✉ **Wallstr 5** ☎ **61 27 78** Ⓤ **Lokalbahnhof** 🚌 **30, 36** 🕘 **5pm-1am** 👶

Germania (2, K10) **$**
Traditional Frankfurt
All are equal in this tiny tavern. Take a seat where you can find one and enjoy the experience. The food is good, the service speedy and friendly. If you're there the day before Shrove Tuesday, don't be surprised if you find everyone dancing on the tables celebrating *Karneval*. Bookings advisable at weekends. No credit cards.
✉ **Textorstr 16**
☎ **61 33 36** Ⓤ **Lokalbahnhof** 🚌 **30, 36**
🕘 **4pm-midnight (Fri-Sun from 11am)** 👶

Henninger Turm (1, H8) $
German
This revolving restaurant at the top of the Henninger brewery building is the only room with a view in Sachsenhausen. The kitchen offers simple German fare; there are better German beers, though. There's a DM5/3 elevator fee. Bookings essential.
✉ **Hainerweg 60-64**
☎ **606 36 01** Ⓤ **Lokalbahnhof** 🚌 **30, 36**
🕘 **12-10pm** 👶 **V**

Martin Moos

Applewine

Even Frankfurters say a taste for 'Main water' has to be acquired. Drinking the juice of pressed apples fresh from an 8-week fermentation goes against the grain. Strangely, applewine is mainly drunk within a 50km radius of Frankfurt. An indication perhaps of how suspiciously other Germans view this sup that dates from the days of Charlemagne? Applewine says much about the character of Frankfurt: abrasive at first, but with a little perseverance you have a friend for life. And, believe me, there's no better thirst-quencher after a long bike ride.

Applewine is served pure, or mixed with mineral water *(sauergespritzt)* or lemonade *(süssgespritzt)*. A small group should have little trouble getting through a 7-glass pitcher, called a *Bembel*. Many restaurants make their own applewine.

Lobster (2, J10) **$$**
International
It may be rustic, but that's about all this establishment has in common with its neighbouring Sachsenhausen applewine taverns, except that none need background music. While guests come for the familiarity of it all, the expert European cuisine is its real *raison d'être*. Fish features strongly, the lamb is irresistible and there's an impressive selection of European wines. Bookings essential. Accepts Visa or Eurocard.
✉ Wallstr 21 ☎ 61 29 20 🚇 Lokalbahnhof 🚌 30, 36 🕘 6pm-1am ♿ V

Maaschanz
(2, H8) **$$$**
French
How could you turn down an invitation to the 'Cognac Consulate' from owner Bruno from La Rochelle? He changes his menu monthly to focus on a particular French region. The wines are all French perfections. And, if that's not enough, there's also live chansons every Saturday night. Bookings advisable. Accepts Eurocard.
✉ Färberstr 75
☎ 62 28 86
🚇 Schweizer Platz
🚌 30, 36, 46 🕘 Tues-Sun 6pm-1am ♿ V

Muschelhaus
(2, J9) **$$**
Seafood
This well worn restaurant looks like it's been transported straight from the docklands of Hamburg. The guests are out-and-out Frankfurters who know their oysters. The catch is delivered twice a week from the Netherlands. Bookings advisable.
✉ Schulstr 36
☎ 62 11 62 🚇 Lokalbahnhof 🚌 30, 36, Eiserner Steg 🕘 Tues-Sat 5.30-11pm ♿

Pinienhof (2, K9) **$$$**
French
This gem is not strictly French, but there are enough exquisite concoctions for it to qualify. It's the warm but dainty surrounds, and the personal touch that make it a pleasure to visit. Perfect for a romantic twosome. Smart dress. Bookings essential. No credit cards.
✉ Gutzkowstr 43
☎ 61 32 37 🚇 Lokalbahnhof; Schweizer Platz 🕘 Tues-Sat 5-11pm, Sun 5-10pm ♿ V

Zum Feuerrädchen
(2, K10) **$**
Traditional Frankfurt
This family-run tavern is one of the cosiest applewine locations in town. The walkway to the entrance is brightly decorated with paintings of Frankfurt in the days of old, and the stained-glass doorway is extremely welcoming. Have a peek into the artfully arranged neighbours' garden. Bookings advisable.
✉ Textorstr 24
☎ 62 13 13
🚇 Lokalbahnhof
🕘 Tues-Fri 3pm-midnight, Sat-Sun 11am-midnight ♿

Zum Gemalten Haus
(1, G7) **$**
Traditional Frankfurt
Tourists of every nation make it down to this applewine tavern as well as the spillover from Wagner next door. Don't be fooled by the 'seen-one-seen-them-all' maxim: each of these taverns has a unique character. Here, colourful wall paintings add warmth to the enclosed yard that becomes an outdoor restaurant in summer. Bookings essential. Accepts Visa or Eurocard.
✉ Schweizer Str 67
☎ 61 45 59
🚇 Schweizer Platz
🕘 Wed-Sun 10am-midnight, Mon & Tues only during trade fairs ♿

Martin Moos

Welcoming sign of a Sachsenhausen applewine tavern

Zum Kanonensteppel
(2, K10) $
Traditional Frankfurt
The name, from a poem by Goethe, refers to tiny men who lived underground and plugged the city's cannons during battles such as the 30 Years' War. Of all the applewine taverns, this is the most charming, and you'll avoid the stampede. Bookings advisable on weekends. No credit cards.
✉ **Textorstr 20**
☎ **61 18 91** Ⓢ **Lokalbahnhof** 🚌 **30, 36**
🕘 **Mon-Sat 11.30-midnight** 🚸

Zum Wagner
(1, G7) $
Traditional Frankfurt
Saturday afternoons here illustrate just how much Frankfurters enjoy a sup in good company. One of Sachsenhausen's oldest and most popular applewine taverns, it's loud, it's jovial, and the kitschy decor is really homy, but get there early or don't come at all. No credit cards.
✉ **Schweizer Str 71**
☎ **61 25 65**
Ⓢ **Schweizer Platz**
🕘 **11am-midnight** 🚸

Martin Moos

Eat, drink and be merry at Zum Wagner.

WESTEND

Bettina-Eck
(2, F1) $$$
European
Excellent dining comes at a squeeze at this popular Westend haunt. Don't leave Frankfurt without trying the asparagus, an applauded summer delicacy. Or try a fish dish from the seafood menu. Steaks and salad are also tops. Bookings essential. Smart dress. Accepts all credit cards.
✉ **Bettinastr 17**
☎ **74 96 52** Ⓢ **Hauptbahnhof** 🚌 **33**
🕘 **Mon-Sat 7am-midnight** 🚸 **V**

Cafe Laumer
(2, C1) $
Cafe
Prepare to sin at this Westend establishment that has all the flair of a Viennese coffee house. The Black Forest Gateau *(Schwarzwälder Kirschtorte)* tastes even better than it looks! But with more than 20 cakes to choose from, where do you start? Also serves breakfast assortments and light meals.
✉ **Bockenheimer Landstr 67** ☎ **72 79 12**
Ⓢ **Westend**
🕘 **7.30am-7pm (Sun from 10am)** 🚸

Gargantua
(2, B3) $$$
Gourmet
Nothing less than a transatlantic merger would warrant a 4-course supper at this gourmet restaurant, but a small-scale joint venture would do for the set lunch. Chef Klaus Trebes is something of a personality on the local gastronomic scene. Bookings essential. Smart dress. Accepts all credit cards.
✉ **Liebigstr 47**
☎ **72 07 18** Ⓢ **Westend** 🕘 **Mon-Fri 12-2.30pm, Mon-Sat 6pm-1am** 🚸 **V**

Jewel of India
(4, C5) $$
Indian
This is the best Indian restaurant in town, and it's only a hop-skip-and-jump from the trade fair grounds. From the mulligatawny soup to the chicken vindaloo, it's an absolute

Dining Like Kings

Well, perhaps not kings, but at least like the Princes of Hessen used to. **Hotel Hessischer Hof** (2, G1; ☎ 754 00), Friedrich-Ebert-Anlage 40, Westend, offers a set lunch menu for DM49 from 12.30-2.30pm daily in its charming Sèvres Restaurant, that includes a 3-course meal with wine and coffee. This is a dining experience not to be missed, set in the hushed, carpeted surrounds of antique chandeliers, age-old dining room furniture and a regal dinner service. German and French cuisine. Not available during trade fairs.

winner. Bookings are essential. All credit cards are accepted.
✉ Wilhelm-Hauff-Str 5 ☎ 75 23 75 🚊 16, 19, Messe 🕒 Sun-Fri 11.30am-2.30pm, daily 6-11.30pm 🚼 V

Joe Pena's (4, B4) **$$**
Mexican
Again, it's not authentic Mexican food, but that's not the point. The trendy young crowd comes to this fun place as much for the Happy Hour cocktails as for the fajitas, which are a tad better than at other would-be Mexican places around. Bookings are advisable.
✉ Robert-Mayer-Str 18 ☎ 705 51 56 Ⓤ Bockenheimer Warte 🕒 Mon-Thurs 5pm-1am, Fri 5pm-2am, Sat 6pm-2am, Sun 6pm-1am V

Morton's Steakhouse
(2, D2) **$$$/$$$$**
Steakhouse
This is arguably the best steakhouse in town, and certainly the most professional. The trendy wines also come at a price. Bookings are advisable. Accepts all credit cards.
✉ Feuerbachstr 11a ☎ 71 03 40 50 Ⓤ Westend; Taunusanlage 🕒 Mon-Fri 12-3pm, Mon-Sat 6pm-midnight 🚼

Ristorante Isoletta
(2, B3) **$$$**
Italian
Sister restaurants in Bad Homburg and Sachsenhausen make this threesome a force to be reckoned with. The concept is upmarket, the service home-style. Try the Pizzabrot for a spicy appetiser. The fresh fish platter makes a wonderful starter, and the pasta mista is the best way to sample some of the countless pasta variations. Bookings are essential. Smart dress. Accepts all credit cards.
✉ Feldbergstr 31 ☎ 72 58 89 Ⓤ Westend 🚌 36 🕒 Mon-Sat 12-2.30pm, 5.30-11.30pm 🚼 V

Sohar (2, F2) **$$**
Kosher
This is Frankfurt's only kosher restaurant, and serves a blend of Jewish and oriental dishes including good salads and some vegetarian selections. Bookings are advisable. Accepts all credit cards.
✉ Savigny Str 66 ☎ 75 23 41 Ⓤ Westend 🕒 Tues-Fri, Sun 12-7.30pm, Sat 1-2pm 🚼 V

Stars & Starlet
(4, D5) **$$$**
International
Convenient for trade fair guests otherwise starved of choice in the immediate vicinity of the fair grounds. A mix of Californian, Asian and European cuisine, the exquisite food comes at exquisite prices, and includes an optical massage from New Yorker Jordan Mozer's star decor. Bookings are advisable. Smart dress. Accepts all credit cards.
✉ Friedrich-Ebert-Anlage 49 ☎ 756 03 00 🚊 16, 19, Messe 🕒 Mon-Thurs 11.30-1am, Fri 11.30-3am, Sat 6pm-3am, Sun only during trade fairs 🚼 V

Surf 'n' Turf
(2, A3) **$$$$**
Seafood & Steak
Brought to you by the same people behind Morton's Steakhouse and housed in the former home of writer Heinrich Hoffmann and composer Engelbert Humperdinck, this establishment carefully retains the classical touch. The walls are lined with dark wood, bottles of vintage wines and intellectual tomes. The menu is exclusively fish and prime beef. Bookings essential.
✉ Grüneburgweg 95 ☎ 72 21 22 Ⓤ Holzhausenstr 🚌 36 🕒 Mon-Fri 12-3pm, Mon-Sat 6pm-midnight 🚼

OTHER SUBURBS

African Queen
(2, K3) $
African/Middle Eastern
This African force was brightening up the Gutleutviertel long before it became trendy to do so, and it's proof that word of mouth works better than advertising when it comes to good food. Spicy Eritrean cooking does the trick here. Bookings advisable.
✉ **Stuttgarter Str 21, Gutleutviertel ☎ 23 29 90 Ⓢ Hauptbahnhof**
🕘 **8-11pm** 🚸 **V**

Ginnheimer Schoene Aussicht (1, C4) **$$**
Traditional Frankfurt
Make the effort and take the 15-minute tram ride out to this garden locale, a world away from the hustle and bustle of the city. Enjoy excellent food under the watchful eye of the 331m-high Europa-Turm TV tower. Bookings advisable. No credit cards.
✉ **Ginnheimer Stadtweg 129, Ginnheim**
☎ 53 28 95
Ⓢ Ginnheim 🚋 16
🕘 **5pm-midnight** 🚸

King Creole
(1, A7) **$$$**
American
There's no lion but plenty of coconut, and of course crabmeat and shrimp – it couldn't call itself Creole without them. It's a bit of a hike out here, but worth it, especially to sit out under the chestnut trees in summer. Bookings advisable. Accepts all credit cards.
✉ **Eckenheimer Landstr 346, Eckenheim ☎ 54 21 72 Ⓢ Marbachweg/ Eckenheimer Landstr**
🕘 **6-11pm** 🚸 **V**

Lohrberg Schänke
(1, A11) **$**
German
Work up an appetite walking up the steep hill from the bus stop, then sit back and enjoy the view of Frankfurt and the Taunus Hills. There's more to this viewpoint than meets the eye (p. 20) The uniformed gents have been serving guests here for years.
✉ **Auf dem Lohr, Seckbach ☎ 47 99 44**
🚌 43, Draisbornstr
🕘 **Tues-Sun 10am-11pm** 🚸 **V**

Worth a Trip

Some of the best spots are located out of town. The following are the highlights.

Die Scheuer (☎ 06192-277 74), Burgstr 2, Hofheim, Ⓢ S2 Hofheim

Drosselbart (☎ 53 43 93), Eschersheimer Landstr 607, Eschersheim, Ⓢ S6 Eschersheim, U1/2/3 Weisser Stein

Frankfurter Haus (☎ 06102-314 66), Darmstädter Landstr 741, Neu-Isenburg, Ⓢ 14 Neu-Isenburg

Momberger (☎ 57 66 66), Alt Heddernheim 13, Heddernheim, Ⓢ U1/2/3 Heddernheim

Speisekammer (☎ 58 77 11), Alt-Heddernheim 41, Heddernheim, Ⓢ U1/2/3 Weisser Stein

Zum Lahmen Esel (☎ 57 39 74), Krautgartenweg 1, Niederursel, Ⓢ U3 Niederursel

Zur Buchscheer (☎ 63 51 21), Schwarzsteinkrautweg 17, Sachsenhausen, Ⓢ S3, S4, Frankfurt-Louisa, 🚋 14

A quirky restaurant in Bad Homburg is the **Kartoffelküche** (☎ 06172-215 00, Audenstr 4, Ⓢ S5 Bad Homburg), which serves up dishes only made from potatoes (yes, even the desserts!). It's located off the main shopping street, Luisenstrasse, and is one of the most popular dining out spots for miles around.

Olivier Strewe

entertainment

While Frankfurt isn't Paris or London, it certainly has its fair share of entertainment. In fact, the Frankfurt Ballet is unparalleled in Europe, and Frankfurt's jazz scene is internationally acclaimed. And venues such as the Alte Oper and Hessischer Rundfunk run highly venerable classical concert series.

Unlike many other German cities, there are a number of foreign-language **theatres**. Much of the German-language theatre involves the local dialect or *Mundart*, and then there's the stalwart municipal theatre, the Schauspielhaus. Several independent companies offer alternative theatre in unusual venues such as the 5-member Dramatische Bühne, which has performed in a park and a church. Cabaret and comedy are also in big demand, with the Tigerpalast vaudeville theatre forging the way.

The **performing arts** also have a strong tradition in Frankfurt. The Mousonturm showcases experimental dance troupes from around the world, and Das TAT has drawn such greats as Robert Wilson. Opera ranges from light-hearted Mozart to heavy-duty modern epics.

What's On?

Unfortunately, there is no regular publication in English about entertainment and nightlife activities. The bi-weekly German-language magazine *Frankfurt Journal* has the market sewn up with its detailed events calendar. The monthly *Prinz* magazine takes a more alternative approach. Freebies *Strandgut* and *Fritz* can be picked up at pubs and cafes around the city. Also keep an eye out for flyers about unofficial parties in strange places. Promoters frequently go around restaurants and bars handing out tickets for entertainment events as well, so keep your eyes and ears peeled.

For every **nightclub** or **bar** that closes, it seems another 3 open up in its place, such is the recent boom in nightlife activities, dominated by slick and trendy forces. But there are also many alternative venues. The independent party scene is one of Germany's most thriving, and Frankfurt is also one of Europe's gay magnets. As the birthplace of techno, Frankfurt has no shortage of dance and trance clubs. So, if it's nonstop entertainment you're looking for, it's possible to party all night long most nights of the week.

Most big-name **bands** play in Frankfurt, usually in the Festhalle or Alte Oper, or out of town in the Stadthalle Offenbach, the Jahrhunderthalle Hoechst or the Hugenottenhalle Neu-Isenburg. But venues are small, and concerts frequently sell out as soon as bookings open.

Martin Moos

All the fun of the fair at Frühlingsdippemess

Special Events

Annual events in and around Frankfurt include the following.

February/March *Fastnacht* – Thursday to Tuesday before Christian Lenten period; parade in Frankfurt (Sun) and Alt-Heddernheim (Tues), *Rosenmontag* parade in Mainz (Mon)
Quartier Latin – Frankfurt University stages an all-night fancy-dress ball

March/April *St Patrick's Day* – celebrated in Frankfurt's 10-odd Irish pubs
Easter Egg Market – Frankfurt Airport Terminal 1 Airport Gallery
International Music Trade Fair – expect some impromptu concerts in pubs and venues
International Jazz Festival – a landmark on Frankfurt's music calendar; international jazz musicians play all over the city

May *Frühlingsdippemess* – carousels and roller-coaster rides at the Eissporthalle grounds, Ratsweg
Nauröder Äppelblütefest – Wiesbaden is first with the season's wine festivals
International Festival of Music, Ballet and Drama – throughout May in Wiesbaden

June *Oldtimer-Rallye* – Wiesbaden shows its fetish for old-timer cars
Wäldchestag – Frankfurters make for the Stadtwald on the Tues after Whitsun with carousels and fairground attractions in the woods
Wilhelmstrassenfest Theatrium – one of Germany's most exclusive street festivals with high-quality jazz and gourmet titbits

June/July *Höchster Schlossfest* – Höchst's castle is the centre of attraction
Offenbacher Mainuferfest – Offenbach celebrates its multicultural character with a festival of the nations at the river
Sommerfest Opernplatz – a week-long gourmet festival at the Opernplatz
Hochheimer Weinfest – one of the region's biggest wine festivals in the historic old town of Hochheim
Der Rhein im Feuerzauber – watch more than 50 rafts, small boats and ships light up the Rhine River with burning flames and fireworks
Sound of Frankfurt – 2-day rock and pop extravaganza on Frankfurt's Zeil
Rosen- und Lichterfest – at Frankfurt Palmengarten, music, fireworks and a kiddies' program

August *Mainfest* – applewine flows from the Fountain of Justice at Römerberg
Rheingauer Weinwoche – 10-day wine festival in Wiesbaden
Rheingauer Weinwoche – 10-day wine festival on the Fressgasse
Museumsuferfest – Frankfurt celebrates its Museums Mile
St Christopher Day – gay parade around Konstablerwache, Grosse Friedberger Strasse and Alte Gasse

September *Laternenfest* – Bad Homburg's unique lantern festival
IAA – Frankfurt international auto show held in odd-numbered years

October *Frankfurt Book Fair* – the world's largest book fair

November/December *Christmas Market* – every day for 4 weeks to 25 December at Paulsplatz and Römerberg
Silvester – watch New Year's Eve fireworks from the Eiserner Steg bridge

BARS & PUBS

Closing Time

Restaurants and bars can serve alcohol until 3am on weekdays and 4am at weekends. That's not to say that everyone does: most pubs wind things down around 1am during the week, and 2am at weekends. Street cafes away from residential areas can stay open to midnight or 1am. Street festivals, a frequent occurrence in summer, usually continue to midnight.

Balalaika (2, J9)
Anita, the bar lady, was singing long before many of her customers were born, as one of the pacesetters in the jazz and blues scene in the swinging 60s. These days she sings a more mellow song in her tiny, candlelit pub. A major attraction during the music trade fair.
✉ Dreikönigstr 30, Sachsenhausen ☎ 61 22 26 Ⓤ Schweizer Platz 🚌 30, 36, 46 ⏲ 8pm-2am (Fri-Sat to 3am)

Bar Oppenheimer
(2, J8-9) This cocktail bar and its next-door neighbour **Orion Bar** go hand in hand. The cocktail shakers have made a real name for themselves around the city.
✉ Oppenheimer Str 41, Sachsenhausen ☎ 62 66 74 Ⓤ Schweizer Platz 🚌 30, 36, 46 ⏲ 8pm-1am (Fri-Sat to 2am)

Bockenheimer Weinkontor (4, B3)
This charming wine bar in spartan surrounds is vintage Frankfurt. Many of the tipplers have been coming here for years working their way through the top-notch wine list.
✉ Schlossstr 92, Bockenheim ☎ 70 20 31 Ⓤ Bockenheimer Warte 🚋 16 ⏲ 8pm-1am (Fri-Sat to 2am)

Opera Outdoors

Frankfurt's most elegant outdoor nightspot has got to be the **Opera** restaurant/bar, the lofty terrace on the 3rd floor of the Alte Oper (2, E5; ☎ 134 02 15), Am Opernplatz. The dramatic view across the square to the banking district is one that can be enjoyed well into the wee small hours: the bar isn't subject to regular closing hours. Open daily from noon till late.

Angela Cullen

Enjoy a view with your brew at Alte Oper.

Cafe Gegenwart
(2, C11) Many Berger Strasse night wanderers don't make it farther than this cafe/bar, the 'daddy' of the Bornheim collection. Located at the bottom of the street, it's the name on everyone's lips. Also a popular gay hangout.
✉ Berger Str 6, Bornheim/Nordend ☎ 497 05 44 Ⓤ Merianplatz ⏲ Sun-Thurs 9-1am, Fri-Sat 10-2am

Chari Vari (2, B13)
There's no need to shoot the piano player – the piano is just for decoration at this bar that serves up a range of German beers and tasty dishes. There's a nice little beer garden too. For all ages and persuasions.
✉ Berger Str 99, Bornheim/Nordend ☎ 49 22 85 Ⓤ Höhenstr ⏲ 6pm-1am (Fri-Sat to 2am)

Eppsteiner Eck (2, C3)
This neighbourhood bar wouldn't be where it is without a touch of

Westend class. It's also a major expat meeting place, and has 'welcome' written all over it.
✉ **Eppsteiner Str 26, Westend ☎ 17 26 03 Ⓢ Westend ⏲ 11-1am (Sun from 5pm)**

Fifth Element (2, D7)
Space-age decor, an art gallery and an upmarket restaurant may seem like a strange combination but it works. This nightspot attracts cinemagoers before and after the show, and a steady stream of 20- and 30-somethings.
✉ **Grosse Eschenheimer Str 20 ☎ 21 99 64 41 Ⓢ Eschenheimer Tor ⏲ 12.30pm-2am (Fri-Sat to 3am)**

Gebrüder Bauer
(2, C13) The Sandweg is showing signs of a burgeoning bar and restaurant culture with this smart bistro leading the way. Guests queue for coveted dining tables, and the wide bar area is good for conversation.
✉ **Sandweg 113, Bornheim ☎ 40 59 27 44 Ⓢ Merianplatz ⏲ Mon-Thurs 6pm-1am, Fri-Sat 6pm-2am, Sun 10-1am**

Havanna Bar (2, G11)
Fickle as Frankfurt's bar scene may be, this bar still manages to be an 'in' place 5 years after its launch. Commendable cocktails and a none-too arrogant crowd.
✉ **Schwanenstr 2, Ostend ☎ 49 56 33 Ⓢ Ostendstr ⏲ 6pm-2am (Fri-Sat to 3am)**

Helium (3, A1)
This bar was hip before

Something Old, Something New

A mix of the trendy and the traditional, the following bars and pubs are also recommended.

An Sibin (2, J10; ☎ 603 21 59) Wallstr 9, Sachsenhausen – one of the more authentic Irish pubs, with occasional Wednesday night music sessions

Aquarium (1, D8; ☎ 46 93 97 77) Rohrbachstr 26, Nordend – a welcoming cafe/bar decked out like an aquarium

Cafe Karin (2, F7; ☎ 29 52 17) Grosser Hirschgraben 28 – an earthy, loud and lively insiders' hangout

Central Park (2, E6; ☎ 91 39 61 46) Kaiserhofstr 12 – good food, good cocktails and beautiful people

Gingko (2, B12; ☎ 49 12 02) Berger Str 81, Bornheim/Nordend – lively atmosphere and good bistro food

Liquid (2, C3; ☎ 71 40 28 28) Liebigstr 13, Westend – an elegant bar with superior bistro food and a hushed atmosphere

MacGowan's (1, D10; ☎ 469 32 23) Berger Str 255, Bornheim – pub grub, live folksy music and rugby and soccer matches on TV. Also at Zeil 10 (2, E8)

O-Ton (2, C11; ☎ 44 00 00) Berger Str (cnr Baumweg 27), Bornheim/Nordend – a trendy cafe/bar with an easygoing atmosphere

Paulaner (2, A11; ☎ 43 15 10) Rotlintstr 28, Nordend – a pillar of Nordend nightlife, with good food, Bavarian beer and trendy decor

Rotlintcafe (1, D8; ☎ 44 96 91) Rotlintstr 60, Nordend – a warm and cosy cafe/bar, a corner of which hosts tensely fought chess games

Martin Moos

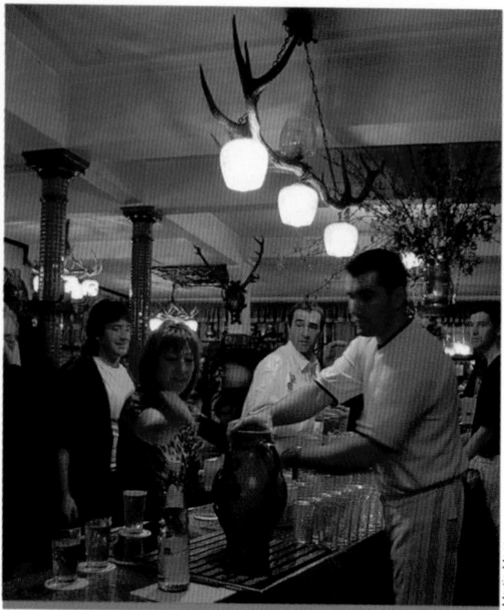

Martin Moos

Try a tiny tipple at a traditional Sachsenhausen bar.

Frankfurters knew what the word meant, and it still pulls in the crowds. It's one of the few places in town where you can be assured of a few people still out at 2am on a Monday or Tuesday. Loud music and strange art on the walls.
✉ **Bleidenstr 7 ☎ 28 70 35 🚇 Hauptwache 🕘 11.30-4am; meals till 2am**

Living (2, G5)
Bankers, brokers and smokers. One of the happening places in town, this is as big as a barn, and sometimes sounds like it. DJs play at weekends, sometimes private parties or cover charge. Sunday night is gay night. It does good business lunches, and Sunday morning jazz in summer.
✉ **Kaiserstr 29 ☎ 242 93 70 🚇 Willy-Brandt-Platz 🕘 Mon-Thurs 11.30-1am, Fri 11.30-3am, Sat 3.30pm-3am, Sun 10-1am**

Lokalbahnhof
(2, K10) Sister to Nordend's Das 21. Jahrhundert (p. 93), this newcomer in the Sachsenhausen area has become a real hotspot. No attention-grabbing decor – plain and simple is the motto.
✉ **Darmstädter Landstr 14, Sachsenhausen ☎ 62 71 62 🚇 Lokalbahnhof 🕘 9-2am (Fri-Sat to 3am)**

Luna Bar (2, E8)
Often voted Frankfurt's coolest bar, this is one not to miss. Excellent cocktails, red gloss and funky music.
✉ **Stiftstr 6 ☎ 29 47 74 🚇 Eschenheimer Tor; Hauptwache 🕘 7pm-2am (Fri-Sat to 3am)**

Palastbar (2, E10)
This wine bar in the cellars of the Tigerpalast cabaret club is a class act to follow a show. But with over 50 cocktail concoctions, and hundreds of wines, cognacs and champagnes to choose from, you may spend more time with your nose in the menu than gazing at the art deco surrounds. This is

Home Brew

Rival breweries Henninger and Binding battle it out in Frankfurt with the latter winning elbows up, judging by brand visibility. But other German beers are available on tap such as the northern German Becks or Jever, or the Cologne darling, Kölsch. There are also 2 micro-breweries who outrate the commercial breweries any day: **Zu den 12 Aposteln** (2, D9; ☎ 28 86 68), Rosenberger Str 1, and **Wäldches** (1, B3; ☎ 52 05 22), Am Ginnheimer Wäldchen 8, Ginnheim.

a meeting place for Frankfurt's establishment, who like a secluded atmosphere.
✉ **Heiligkreuzgasse 16-20 ☎ 92 00 22 92**
Ⓜ **Konstablerwache**
🕓 **Tues-Sun 5pm-2am**

Rote Bar (3, D5)
Fans come from far and wide to visit the toilets at Rote Bar. I'll say no more, save that this cocktail bar enjoys cult status in Frankfurt, which is why it only needs to open 3 or 4 hours a day.
✉ **Mainkai 7**
☎ **29 35 33**
Ⓜ **Konstablerwache, Römer** 🕓 **10pm-1am (Fri-Sat to 2am)**

Strandperle (2, H8)
A gem of a cocktail bar built into the south pier of the Eiserner Steg footbridge. There were real architects at play here: try and find the rest rooms. Strandperle's walk-in/walk-out design ensures a transient crowd and an engaging atmosphere.
✉ **Schaumainkai 17/ Eiserner Steg, Sachsenhausen ☎ 60 32 56 67**
Ⓜ **Römer** 🚌 **46**
🕓 **6pm-2am (Fri-Sat to 3am)**

Studio Bar (3, A1)
It's the summer rooftop terrace that draws a party crowd to this funky bar right at the centre of town. Inside, the bouncy leather seats and 70s touch are too hip to be cool. Pity management's so keen to sweep you out the door as soon after 1am as possible. The club sandwiches are superb.
✉ **Katharinenpforte 6**
☎ **13 37 92 25**
Ⓜ **Hauptwache**
🕓 **Mon-Sat 5pm-1am**

Taboo (2, C4)
The bright orange walls and blue leather seats knock you for six. If you're depressed going in, you'll come out beaming. This is where yuppie Westenders hang out, morning or evening. The brunches are superb.
✉ **Unterlindau 69, Westend ☎ 97 20 36 61** Ⓜ **Westend; Alte Oper** 🕓 **11-1am**

Hot Spots

Three thoroughly different but unmissable spots include **Cafe Klemm** (4, B4; ☎ 97 07 45 12), Kiesstr 41, a designer cafe/bar that may seem out of place in student Bockenheim but is always teeming; **Cafe Läuft** (1, D8; ☎ 43 59 85), Rohrbachstr 26, the ever-popular, grungy Nordend haunt; and **Cafe Klatsch** (2, A15; ☎ 490 97 09), Mainkurstr 29, a perfectly homy cafe/bar in Bornheim.

Martin Moos

Bars, taverns and clubs beckon in Sachsenhausen.

LIVE MUSIC VENUES

Batschkapp
This concert venue has been going for over 25 years, and is a real Frankfurt institution. DJs play a pogo-dancing selection of 80s and independent artists on Friday and Saturday nights (10pm-4am).
✉ Maybachstr 24, Eschersheim ☎ 95 21 84 10 @ info@batschkapp.de Ⓤ Eschersheim; Weisser Stein $ DM14-28

Brotfabrik (1, C2)
Ethnic jazz and one-world music concerts are held in this old bread factory. A big attraction is the salsa disco every Wednesday night (9.45pm-2am). Learn this erotic Latin American body-weaving at the 2hr workshops (6.45-8.45pm) just before the disco starts (phone to check price).
✉ Bachmannstr 2-4, Hausen ☎ 789 55 13 @ kultur@brotfabrik.de Ⓤ Grosse Nelkenstr; Fischstein $ DM16-24

Dreikönigskeller
(2, H9) This Sachsenhausen institution holds 40 at a pinch in a tiny cellar, and always knows how to surprise. You could find a

Martin Moos
Choices, choices

bunch of 20-year-olds mixing their own grooves, an ageing Mick Jagger type drumming up some nostalgia, German Schlagermusik, or experimental free jazz.
✉ Färberstr 71, Sachsenhausen ☎ 62 92 73 Ⓤ Römer; Schweizer Platz 🚌 46 🕘 from 8pm $ DM10-20

King Kamehameha Club (1, E11)
The 80s house band on Thursday is so popular the queue stretches for miles outside the door. Bands also play salsa and Afro-Cuban rhythms. This relative newcomer has become a major trendsetter in Frankfurt nightlife. There's live music Tuesday to Thursday, disco nights Friday and Saturday. Go early or you'll be turned away at the door.
✉ Hanauer Landstr 192, Ostend ☎ 40 59 11 94, tickets ☎ 94 41 10 15 🚊 11, Schwedlerstr 🕘 Tues-Wed 6pm-2am, Thurs-Sat 6pm-4am $ DM10

Nachtleben (2, E9)
This popular concert venue has a fetish for Britpop, folk and rock. The cafe at street level is a regular meeting place, while the nightclub downstairs offers live bands early in the week, and well-known local DJs at weekends. It attracts a young, grunge set.
✉ Kurt-Schumacher-Str 45/Konstablerwache ☎ 206 50, 29 69 29 Ⓤ Konstablerwache 🕘 Mon-Wed 11.30-2am, Thurs-Sat 11.30-4am, Sun 7pm-2am $ DM10-24

Sinkkasten (2, E8)
Only a hermit would never have heard of Sinkkasten. Right bang in the city centre just off the Zeil, this is one of Frankfurt's oldest concert and dance venues, and you can't help but fall into it at some stage. Its low ceilings and cinema seats set the atmosphere for the jazz, funk and rock bands that play here. Friday and Saturday night discos attract 80s and Weather Girls freaks.
✉ Brönnerstr 5 ☎ 28 03 85 Ⓤ Konstablerwache 🕘 8pm-3am $ DM7-10

Naked George

If you happen to spot a middle-aged man wearing nothing but Birkenstock sandals and a Walkman sitting around the cafes and bars of Sachsenhausen, don't be surprised. *Der nackte Jörg*, or naked George, is the nickname given to this local character, who has shed his clothing for political protest, claiming he stands for the 'naked truth'. He's probably the most arrested man in Frankfurt, but the police have given up on apprehending him.

DANCE CLUBS

Cooky's (2, F6)
Once a frontrunner among Frankfurt's live concert venues, this small nightclub now just has DJs playing nightly, mostly house and dance classics. Still, it's pretty central.
✉ **Am Salzhaus 4**
☎ **28 76 62**
Ⓜ **Hauptwache**
🕘 **Sun-Thurs 11pm-5am (closed Tues), Fri-Sat 10pm-end**
$ **DM10-12**

Das 21. Jahrhundert (2, C7) It serves excellent bistro food, but it's not a bistro; it has a few bar stools at a funky counter, but it's not really a bar. And DJs play loud house and dance music most nights, but it's not a club. In fact, it's typical of a number of independent venues around Frankfurt that arrange their own parties, and have a loyal following.
✉ **Oeder Weg 21, Nordend** ☎ **55 67 46**
Ⓜ **Eschenheimer Tor**
🕘 **9-2am (Fri-Sat to 3am)**

Deelight (2, E8)
An Indian theme runs through it. The front room is a bar with wooden floors, stonework and ominous candles; the back room stars local DJs. Jammed to bursting point Friday and Saturday, it tends to be empty early in the week.
✉ **Holzgraben 9**
☎ **13 37 66 24**
Ⓜ **Hauptwache; Konstablerwache**
🕘 **5pm-4am**

Divine (2, E6)
DJ nights in a snakepit-cum-spaceship. Ten out of 10 for imaginative decor, but just what it's meant to be is a mystery. The music is hip, and the bar staff are spot-on. The caipirinhas will knock you for six.
✉ **Kaiserhofstr 13-15**
☎ **28 99 77** Ⓜ **Alte Oper; Hauptwache**
🕘 **5pm-end**

Dorian Gray (5, C6)
Once the pride of Frankfurt's techno scene,

Singled Out

Frankfurt is Singles City. Over 50% of households are 1-person households, and the city's nightlife is very much singles-oriented. It's easy to meet people, and women on their own rarely get hassled. But the nightlife scene is also very fickle, with trends changing almost with the weather, so it's difficult to keep up with what's hip and what's out.

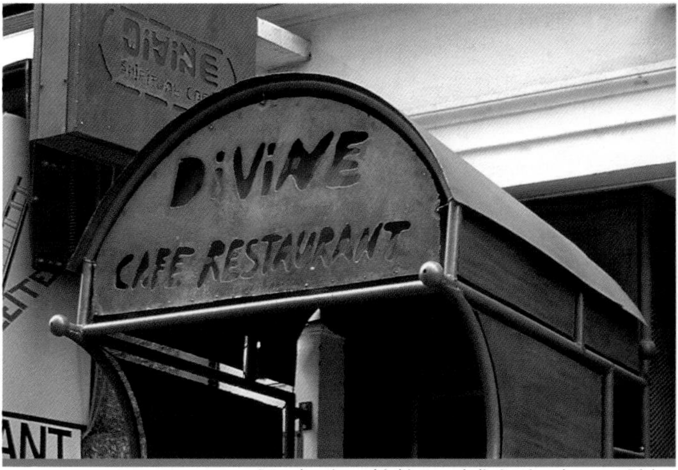

Martin Moos

DJs, dancing, drinking and distinctive decor at Divine

where DJ Talla and Sven Väth cut their teeth, this now has to compete with the growing number of city centre venues, and has lost some of its appeal (although it's only a 12-minute journey to the airport from the city centre).
✉ **Hall C, Frankfurt Airport ☎ 69 02 21 21**
Flughafen ⌚ Fri-Sat 10pm-end

Frankfurter Schule (2, B6) Black walls, a bright blue and red neon bar area, and DJs turning vinyl in dizzying funk and soul motion. For students and thinkers.
✉ **Fichardstr 62, Nordend**
☎ **59 79 19 43**
Grüneburgweg
⌚ **8pm-3am**

Galerie (2, H2)
Women have it easier than men getting in to this 90s-style mainstream dance club. Bouncers at the door will escort you to your car afterwards. Dance floor, house and triphop.
✉ **Düsseldorfer Str 1-7, Bahnhofsviertel**
☎ **23 01 71**
Hauptbahnhof
⌚ **Thurs-Sat 10pm-end, Mon 9pm-end**

Odeon (2, D10)
Housed in the former Bethmann Museum Pavilion in the park, this is one of the most picturesque dance clubs, and has a secluded summer garden. 27-Up Club Fri guarantees no techno, no teenies and no sandals. Bouncers can be contrary.
✉ **Seilerstr 34 ☎ 97 46 05 55 Konstablerwache; Zoo**
⌚ **6pm-end**

Opium (2, F6)
This ambitious newcomer on the local scene combines food with dance. It's a classic nightclub that goes for the upmarket bracket.
✉ **Salzhaus 4**
☎ **13 37 60 72**
Hauptwache
⌚ **Thurs 10pm-2am, Fri-Sat 10pm-end**

Ostklub (2, F15)
Founded by local nightlife guru Hans Romanov, this mini club is little more than a shack but is a major hangout on the independent scene. Local and European DJs play house, Britpop and rock to an insider crowd.
✉ **Hanauer Landstr 99, Ostend ☎ 49 87 03**
Ostbahnhof
⌚ **Tues-Sun 9 or 10pm-3am**

Ostparkstrasse 25 (O25) (1, F9) Once you've found this place, below street level in an old wall, you can party all night long, with no neighbours to worry about. House and drums 'n' bass. Saturday night James Fast Orchestra.
✉ **Ostparkstr 25, Ostend ☎ 79 30 63 58**
Ostbahnhof
⌚ **Wed-Sat 11pm-end**

Space Place (1, H4)
Techno and chill-out. This place is successfully trying to do for the west docklands what the Hanauer Landstrasse venues are doing for the east end. It also runs a series of beach parties in summer. Advisable to use taxis.
✉ **Gutleutstr 294, Gutleutviertel**
☎ **24 24 61 21**
Galluswarte ⌚ Fri-Sat 10pm-end

Stereo Bar (2, J10)
This funky little cellar club describes the music it pumps out as sonic trash. Expect anything from video shows to dizzying strobes. The orange walls set it apart from other Frankfurt nightclubs, many of which go for dark, ominous tones.
✉ **Abtsgässchen 7, Sachsenhausen**
☎ **61 71 16**
Lokalbahnhof
30, 36 ⌚ Wed-Sat 10.30pm-end

The Cave (2, E8)
With everything from Neue Deutsche Welle (remember Nina's '99 Red Balloons'?) to Depeche Mode revivals and Gothic trance, and complete with chill-out room, this stone cellar is perfect to contain the throbbing beats.
✉ **Brönnerstr 11**
☎ **28 38 08**
Konstablerwache
⌚ **Mon-Fri 9pm-4am, Sat-Sun 10pm-6am**

U60311 (2, F6)
The name stands for Underground + the postal code of this techno venue, and it's where the father of techno, Sven Väth, performs. The concrete structure of this converted old subway station makes it perfect for the breakneck beats per minute that he and his compatriots pump out. The entrance is an unassuming cabin-like structure at Rossmarkt.
✉ **Am Rossmarkt**
☎ **297 06 03 11**
Hauptwache
⌚ **Thurs-Sat 10pm-end**

JAZZ & BLUES

Blues & Beyond
(2, A14) With its tiled floor and neon lights, this blues concert venue doesn't immediately strike a chord with its decor. The same can't be said about the blues bands that play here, however. The owner has been in the international music scene for years and knows how to pick them. Jam sessions are held on Monday.
✉ **Berger Str 159, Bornheim ☎ 94 59 27 26, 134 04 00**
Ⓤ Bornheim Mitte
🕘 8pm-3am Ⓢ DM7-20

Jazzkeller (2, E5)
This is where it all started, Frankfurt's jazz scene in the roaring 50s. Things are a lot more civilised these days, and paying guests take their concerts extremely seriously. All that changes at the Swingin' Latin Funky discos on Wednesday and Friday as the party mood breaks out. Concerts are held Wednesday and Saturday.
✉ **Kleine Bockenheimer Str 18a ☎ 28 85 37**
Ⓤ Alte Oper; Hauptwache 🕘 8pm-3am
Ⓢ DM20

Mampf (2, C13)
This smoky little jazz venue is so delicious it seems almost a pity to publicise it. It only fits about 20, but the world and his dog are there. The concerts (on Wednesday, Saturday and Sunday at 8.30pm) are always excellent, and the tiny kitchen produces the most delectable *Grüne Sosse* and spaghetti bolognese.
✉ **Sandweg 64, Bornheim ☎ 44 86 74**
Ⓤ Merianplatz
🕘 7pm-1am (Fri-Sat to 2am)

Steinern Haus
(2, J10) Swing and light jazz is the tonic in this mellow stone cellar. Concerts are held Friday and Saturday; your first drink costs DM5 extra as admission fee.
✉ **Klappergasse 3, Sachsenhausen**
☎ 62 68 00
Ⓤ Lokalbahnhof
🚊 14 🕘 Tues-Sun 8pm-2am

Kim Grant

Frankfurt's jazz scene has a proud tradition.

Martin Moos

Blues fans are well catered for at Blues & Beyond.

CLASSICAL MUSIC & OPERA

Alte Oper (2, E5)
The Hessischer Rundfunk radio symphony orchestra, the Frankfurter Museumsorchester and the Ensemble Modern give regular classical concerts here. The London Symphony Orchestra or the Chamber Orchestra of Europe also appear occasionally, and Anne-Sophie Mutter, Nigel Kennedy and the Alban Berg Quartett are frequent guests.
✉ **Am Opernplatz**
☎ **134 04 00** Ⓤ **Alte Oper**

Church & Chamber Music

The **Main-Barockorchester** (☎ 06447-74 79) and the **Amt für Kirchenmusik** (☎ 247 71 90) can provide information about church and chamber music in the Katharinenkirche and the Karmeliterkloster; or pick up leaflets at the venues themselves.

Hessischer Rundfunk Sunday Lunchtime Concerts (1, C6)
One Sunday every month the HR radio station offers a gourmet culinary event for DM45: classical music and Sunday lunch in the *Sendesaal*, or recording studios, and the HR-Restaurant. Lunch tickets can be booked up to the Wednesday before the concert, at the latest.
✉ **Funkhaus am Dornbusch, Bertramstr 8, Nordend** ☎ **134 04 00** Ⓤ **Dornbusch**

Hochschule für Musik & Darstellende Kunst (2, D7)
The students at this music college treat the public to recitals at irregular intervals. Pick up a flyer from the college for details.
✉ **Eschersheimer Landstr 29-39, Nordend/Westend**
☎ **154 00 70**
Ⓤ **Eschenheimer Tor**

Oper Frankfurt
(2, H5) From Puccini to Mozart and Wagner, the Frankfurt opera performs the classics as well as modern opera in the 'new' opera house (it's now decades old). The subscription series includes a 'learn about opera' selection of 4 tickets.
✉ **Untermainanlage 11**
☎ **21 23 73 33**
Ⓤ **Willy-Brandt-Platz**

BALLET & PERFORMANCE ART

Das TAT Bockenheimer Depot
(4, A5) This avant-garde centre for performance art and theatrical events is a major Frankfurt attraction. The Frankfurt Ballet performs here regularly, and the Ballet's director, William Forsythe, is also the artistic director for Das TAT. Multimedia shows, coproductions with international artists, and dance festivals are just a taste of what's on offer.
✉ **Bockenheimer Depot, Bockenheim**
☎ **21 23 79 99, 21 23 75 55** ⓔ **www.frankfurt-ballett.de** Ⓤ **Bockenheimer Warte**

Frankfurt Ballet
(2, H5) William Forsythe's modern ballet troupe performs at 3 venues in the city: the Schauspiel and the Oper at Willy-Brandt-Platz,

Tickets

The main ticket outlets are **Frankfurt Ticket** (2, E5; ☎ 134 04 00), Alte Oper, Mon-Fri 8am-8pm, Sat 8am-7pm, Sun 11am-7pm; **Best Tickets** (2, E8; ☎ 91 39 76 21), Zeilgalerie, Mon-Fri 10am-8pm, Sat 9am-4pm; **Journal Ticket Shop** (2, E7; ☎ 44 10 49), Hauptwache Passage, Mon-Fri 10am-7pm, Sat 9am-4pm; and **Theaterkasse Hertie** (2, E9; ☎ 29 48 48), Zeil 90, Mon-Fri 9.30am-8pm, Sat 9am-4pm. Note: Concert/event tickets often include the price of the return subway fare to the performance.

The Frankfurt Ballet and the Oper Frankfurt offer last-minute tickets at reductions of up to 50%. Check the box office an hour before the show.

as well as Das TAT at Bockenheimer Depot. The dancers also tour every summer, and some have begun to make a name for themselves as artists in their own right.
✉ **Untermainanlage 11** ☎ **21 23 79 99, 21 23 75 55** **www.frankfurt-ballett.de** **Willy-Brandt-Platz**

Mousonturm (2, C13)
This is a premier venue for modern dance and performance art with acts from all over the world treading its boards. It's far from soap opera, even if the building was once a soap factory. The Bar M Kantine is a wonderful bistro that attracts a theatrical crowd.
✉ **Waldschmidtstr 4, Bornheim/Ostend** ☎ **40 58 95 20** **Merianplatz; Zoo**

Martin Moos
The innovative and internationally renowned TAT

THEATRE & COMEDY

English Theater
(2, H4) This small English-language theatre struggled for years, trying to make ends meet until overnight success with a production of *The Rocky Horror Show* in the late 1990s. It hasn't looked back since. It does 4 or 5 shows a year, then closes for summer.
✉ **Kaiserstr 52, Bahnhofsviertel** ☎ **24 23 16 20** **www.virtualcity.de/englishtheater** **Hauptbahnhof**

Galli Theater (1, D3)
Children will love the morning clown theatre and the afternoon fairy-tale theatre. A knowledge of German is needed for many of the evening theatre shows for the bigger kiddies, but there are also music events at this house of satire and wit.
✉ **Basaltstr 23, Bockenheim** ☎ **970 97 80** **Leipziger Str**

Internationales Theater Frankfurt
(2, F12) Six foreign-language amateur theatres in one. The English Pocket Theater vies for attention with Ibero-American, Spanish, Russian, German and Japanese theatres. It's a beautiful stage and performance hall, but seems a little lost in this out-of-the-way passage. There are also art exhibitions and musical recitals.
✉ **Hanauer Landstr 5-7/Zoo Passage, Ostend** ☎ **499 09 80** **ww.Internationales-Theater.de** **Ostendstr; Zoo**

Neues Theater Höchst (5, C6)
Language may sometimes be a problem, but with its range of cabaret, music and clowning around, this theatre in Höchst regularly brings the house down without a word. It also runs some English comedy acts, so check the program for details.
✉ **Emmerich-Joseph-Str 46a, Höchst**

☎ 339 99 90, 33 99 99 33 Ⓤ Höchst

Tigerpalast (2, E10)
It's often easier to get tickets outside Frankfurt than in it for this high-class vaudeville theatre with acts from around the world, even though there are 2 shows a day. Set in a one-time church, the stage is small, and some of the artistes perform high above the audience. Local politicians often get invited to sit on a bench perched above the spectators so they can be ridiculed by the compere (all in good fun).
✉ **Heiligkreuzgasse 16-20 ☎ 92 00 22 50, 920 02 20 Ⓤ Konstablerwache ⌚ Tues-Sat 8 & 11.30pm, Sun 4 & 8pm**

We're All Going On A Summer Holiday

You'll find this hard to believe, but some Frankfurt theatres and entertainment venues take a summer holiday break. The reason being that *many* German families make for the Mediterranean once school holidays hit. The mass exodus is so extreme that school holidays are staggered between the 16 federal states to alleviate traffic jams, but even still, 10hr motorway stoppages are quite the norm during these periods.

CINEMAS

Cinemaxx (1, G13)
This new movie theatre complex in Offenbach, right on the border with Frankfurt, is less than 10 minutes from Konstablerwache on the S8 line. It shows films in English on Monday.
✉ **Berliner Str 210, Offenbach ☎ 80 90 41 44 Ⓤ Ledermuseum**

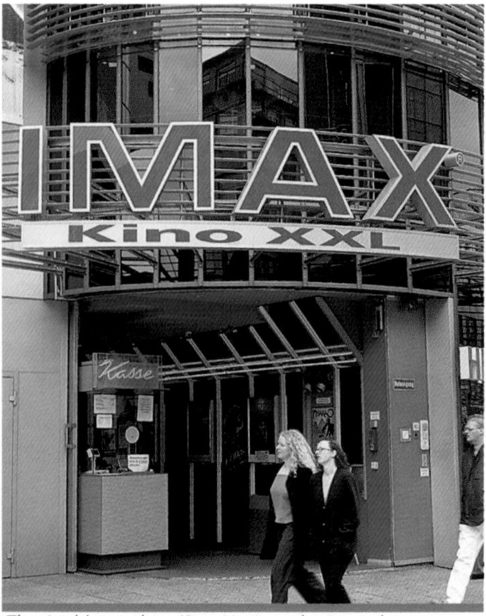

Martin Moos
They're bigger than 'Ben Hur', at the Imax theatre.

Deutsches Filmmuseum (2, J7)
Often showing film premieres and directors' presentations, the movie theatre here specialises in *auteur* films and retrospectives, and releases a new program monthly. The museum houses the most extensive collection of German film available and the library and archive are open to the public at certain times of the day. (☎ 21 23 88 41, 21 23 36 23).
✉ **Schaumainkai 41, Sachsenhausen ☎ 21 23 88 30 Ⓤ Schweizer Platz; Willy-Brandt-Platz 🚌 46**

Imax (2, E8)
This 400-sq-m screen arrived in mid-1999 to enhance the Zeilgalerie shopping mall with 3D and special Imax cinematography. It often suffers technical hitches.
✉ **Zeilgalerie ☎ 13 38 48 21 Ⓤ Hauptwache ⌚ screenings every**

hour 11am-midnight ⓢ DM25

Orfeo's Erben (4, C3)
This place combines a trendy cafe with a cinema showing cult movies, Third World cinema and Japanese film, and attracting a hip collection of Jim Jarmusch fans. There are often subtitles but check beforehand.
✉ **Hamburger Allee 45, Bockenheim ☎ 70 76 91 00 Ⓤ 16, 19 Messe**

Turmpalast (2, D7)
Seven cinemas all showing the latest releases in English. On Sunday night the queue stretches all the way down the street. No air-conditioning, but that doesn't seem to bother the masses that congregate.
✉ **Eschenheimer Turm**
☎ **28 17 87**
Ⓤ **Eschenheimer Tor**

Werkstatt Kino Mal Seh'n (2, A9)
This is one of a number of *Programmkinos* or art-house movie theatres around town that show off-centre art movies, sometimes in English. Check flyers or *Strandgut* or *Fritz* magazines for details. Also nurtures a club of dedicated Emma Peel fans with regular showings of *The Avengers*.
✉ **Adlerflychtstr 6, Nordend**
☎ **597 08 45**
Ⓤ **Musterschule**

GAY & LESBIAN FRANKFURT

Frankfurt has an active and open gay community that, while much smaller than other European gay centres, stages a number of events including the annual St Christopher Day parade and the city's version of the Gay Olympics.

The area with the highest concentration of gay bars is off the Konstablerwache: Stephanstrasse, Schäfergasse, Alte Gasse, Elephantengasse and Bleichstrasse – but there are many others dotted around that attract a mixed gay and straight clientele. Sundays are big in the gay calendar. As well as the exclusively gay clubs, many of Frankfurt's dance venues arrange regular gay nights.

Blue Angel (2, D8)
Any night of the week there'll be a party going on here. Sunday and Monday nights are usually dedicated to German *Schlagermusik*, or Tom Jones-'Delilah'-type music.
✉ **Brönnerstr 17**
☎ **28 27 72**
Ⓤ **Konstablerwache**
🕘 **Mon-Tues 11pm-4am, Wed-Sun 9-4am**

Cafe Lilliput (3, B1)
Hidden in the Sandhof-Passage at Liebfrauenberg, this delightful cafe has one of Frankfurt's most beautiful and secluded gardens, which has to be seen to be believed. This is a gem, especially on Saturday afternoon.
✉ **Sandhof-Passage**
☎ **28 57 27** Ⓤ **Hauptwache** 🕘 **10am-midnight (Sun from 2pm)**

Central (2, D9)
Central has been leading the way in the gay scene for over a decade, and bursts at the seams during trade fairs. This dimly lit place also has its quiet moments, though it's not evident when!
✉ **Elephantengasse 11-13** ☎ **29 29 26**
Ⓤ **Konstablerwache**
🕘 **Mon-Thurs 8pm-1am, Fri-Sat 8pm-2am**

Harvey's (2, B11)
This odd-shaped, high-

Meet the Family

Lucky's Manhattan (2, D9; ☎ 28 49 19), Schäfergasse 27 and **Switchboard** (2, D9; ☎ 28 35 35), Alte Gasse 36, are 2 gay bars that most newcomers hear about or head for on arrival. This is also where you can pick up information about the scene in Frankfurt. The **Continental Bath House** (2, D9; ☎ 28 27 57), Alte Gasse 5, open 2pm-4am (Fri-Sat to 8am), is the biggest gay sauna and leisure facility.

ceilinged corner bar, looking like Dame Edna's living room, is the perfect setting for flouncing around, and boy, do they. It's a long-established location on the gay map, but attracts a mixed crowd.
✉ **Bornheimer Landstr 64, Nordend ☎ 49 73 03 Ⓤ Merianplatz 🚋 12 🕗 10-1am (Fri-Sat to 2am)**

Lagerhaus (2, J11)
The finger-food platter is to die for, but all of the creative dishes are tantalising here, one of the most popular spots for gay and straight to meet. It brightens up this corner of Sachsenhausen no end with its frescoes and colour.
✉ **Dreieichstr 45, Sachsenhausen ☎ 62 85 52 Ⓤ Lokalbahnhof 🚋 14 🕗 10-2am**

LOFT House (1, F10)
It's the biggest gay club in town with countless rooms and dance floors decked out in a different decor almost every week. The main event is the Saturday night Loveball with international dance bands and mostly techno and house music.
✉ **Hanauer Landstr 181-185, Ostend ☎ 943 44 80 🚋 11, Schwedlerstr 🕗 Sat 10pm-end**

Stall (2, E8)
Less of the party and more of the underground scene.
✉ **Stiftstr 22 ☎ 29 18 80 Ⓤ Konstablerwache**

Zum Schwejk (2, D9)
Meet the Marianne Rosenberg fan club! This is *the* place to go to put you in a good mood for the evening, even if it's a tight squeeze in the door. It only holds a handful. Highly recommended.
✉ **Schäfergasse 20 ☎ 29 31 66 Ⓤ Konstablerwache 🕗 Mon-Thurs 11-1am, Fri-Sat 11-2am, Sun 3pm-1am**

SPECTATOR SPORT

Frankfurt Lions
(1, D11) The Lions may be up and down in the German ice-hockey league, but they've got some of the most supportive fans around. Many Scandinavians and Canadians play in the premier league, as the clubs try to raise the standard of ice-hockey in Germany.
✉ **Eissporthalle, Ratsweg 4, Ostend ☎ 405 88 40 for info, 134 04 00 for tickets Ⓤ Eissporthalle 🕗 season Oct-Mar**

Eintracht Frankfurt
The club is bankrupt, and players and fans are deserting in droves, but this local soccer club will survive to tell the tale. This is what soccer's all about.
✉ **Waldstadion, Niederrad 🚋 19, Stadion**

Martin Moos

Must-read material for the football faithful

Frankfurt Galaxy
It's a short season, but the men in shoulder pads make the most of it. But real football fans won't want to know. The NFL Europe is light years from America's Superbowl. Still, it goes down well among the uninitiated.
✉ **Waldstadion, Niederrad ☎ 01805-26 62 16, ☎ Best Tickets 202 28 🚋 19, Stadion 🕗 season Apr-June**

Pferderennbahn Niederrad (1, K4)
Frankfurt's answer to Royal Ascot is just a 15-minute tram ride from Sachsenhausen. Also referred to as Galopprennbahn, it holds races most Sundays.
✉ **Schwarzwaldstr, Niederrad ☎ Best Tickets 202 28 🚋 19, Rennbahnstr 🕗 season Mar-Oct $ entrance fee DM12**

places to stay

Of the 3 million-odd overnight visitors Frankfurt gets every year, only 30% are 'regular' tourists. Not surprising, given the city's status as an international trade fair centre. Apply Murphy's Law and you will conclude that your chances of finding a hotel room here are in direct proportion to the number of major trade fairs happening at the time.

Martin Moos

Room Rates

The categories in this chapter indicate the regular cost per night for a standard double room:

Top End	from DM300
Mid-Range	DM180-299
Budget	below DM180

Martin Moos

From homely to high-rise

Frankfurt's clock ticks according to its trade fairs. Regular hotel prices almost double at these times, and rooms during events like the International Book Fair in October or the IAA auto show every 2nd September are often booked out years in advance. At off-peak times, the 163 hotels and 22,000 beds are more than enough to cater for the average daily influx of 8000 visitors.

While most hotels have a 2-night weekend special rate, cut-rate budget accommodation is hard to come by, as is true for all major cities in Germany. Breakfast is usually included in the room rates, and bathrooms are usually en suite and often with a bathtub. Prices can vary greatly from regular rates so check when booking.

Styles vary (even if Hiltons look the same all over the world), and Frankfurt has some unique hotels that carry a weight of tradition, like the Hessischer Hof, which accommodated the Princes of Hessen, or the Frankfurter Hof, which dates back to 1876. There are clusters of hotels in the Bahnhofsviertel, Westend and city centre and none is too far from the action.

Bookings

The Frankfurt tourist office offers free advance telephone and written hotel reservations (☎ 21 23 08 08, fax 21 24 05 12, ⓔ info@tcf.frankfurt.de, www.frankfurt.de), but charges a DM5 same-day fee at Tourist Information Hauptbahnhof near the ticket hall at the main train station (Monday to Friday 8am-9pm, Saturday and Sunday 9am-6pm). Trade fair guests can make room reservations directly in the Torhaus, Level 3, in the fair grounds.

TOP END

Alexander Am Zoo (2, D14) Part of the Best Western chain, this swanky hotel is situated in a quiet street near the zoo. But it's not completely away from it all: the Berger Strasse, swarming with people at its countless street cafes on summer evenings, is a stone's throw away. Another boon is the exclusive Italian restaurant Danilo next door.
✉ **Waldschmidtstr 59-61, Ostend ☎ 94 96 00; fax 94 96 07 20 @ info@alexander.bestwestern.de Ⓤ Zoo**

Arabella Sheraton Grand Hotel (2, D9) This is Frankfurt's classiest address, and has bedded pop stars and royalty in its day. The hotel bar isn't as sad as many others and, far from being incidental, the evening music program is actually quite laudable.
✉ **Konrad-Adenauer-Str 7 ☎ 298 10; fax 298 18 10 @ Grand Hotel.frankfurt@ArabellaSheraton.com Ⓤ Konstablerwache**

Martin Moos
The historic Hotel Hessischer Hof

Comfort aplenty at the Alexander Am Zoo

Hilton Hotel (2, D6) Much like any other Hilton, this one has a little piece of Frankfurt built in, namely the swimming pool in The Wave fitness centre, the site of the former municipal baths. The hotel rooms to the back look out onto the Bockenheimer Anlage, part of the green belt of parkland encircling the inner city.
✉ **Hochstr 4 ☎ 133 80 00; fax 13 38 13 38 @ fom_frankfurt@hilton.com; www.hilton.com Ⓤ Eschenheimer Tor**

Hotel Harheimer Hof Get in touch with nature at the Harheimer Hof situated near the Nidda tributary just a 30-minute city-rail ride north of Frankfurt. The Nidda (p. 28) is idyllic for an evening stroll, and Harheim is a popular destination for cyclists in summer. The hotel has its own gelateria to help guests cool down in summer, and in winter the marble floor-heating in each bathroom keeps the toes warm.
✉ **Alt-Harheim 11, Harheim ☎ 06101-40 50; fax 40 54 11 @ harheimerhof@t-online.de Ⓢ Berkersheim**

Hotel Hessischer Hof (2, G1) One of the top luxury hotels, much of the furniture and ornamentation here belonged to the Princes of Hessen. Service is unflinching, right down to the toll-free numbers in the UK (☎ 0800 181 123), US/Canada (☎ 800 223 6800), New York City (☎ 212 838 31 10), Hong Kong (☎ 800 25 18) and Japan (☎ 3 52 10 51 31). Sound-proofed windows block out the sound of traffic and construction so commonplace around Frankfurt.
✉ **Friedrich-Ebert-Anlage 40, Westend ☎ 75 40 29 11; fax 75 40 29 12 @ info@hessischer-hof.de; www.hessischer-hof.de 🚋 16, 19, Messe**

Hotel Intercontinental
(2, J4) With 469 rooms, the Interconti has a task to keep its guests entertained in the evenings. It does this remarkably well with live music every night at the Daxx bar, and excellent bistro dining at Signatures, popular also with regular Frankfurters. The hotel is close to the opera and Frankfurt Ballet and not too far from some of the liveliest nightlife spots.
✉ Wilhelm-Leuschner-Str 43, Bahnhofsviertel ☎ 260 50; fax 25 24 67 e frankfurt@interconti.com Ⓤ Hauptbahnhof; Willy-Brandt-Platz

Le Meridien Parkhotel (2, J4)
Built in 1905, this hotel has 296 luxury rooms and is one of the nobler establishments in the Bahnhofsviertel. It's within walking distance of the opera, Frankfurt Ballet and the English Theater.
✉ Wiesenhüttenplatz 28-38, Bahnhofsviertel ☎ 269 70 ; fax 269 78 84 e gm1275@forte-hotel.com; www.lemeridien-hotels.com Ⓤ Hauptbahnhof

Miramar (3, B3)
Situated between the Dom and the Zeil, this 4-star hotel has 39 rooms, all air-conditioned. From this convenient location, a stroll across the Eiserner Steg bridge to Sachsenhausen is the best way to work up an appetite for some local grub.
✉ Berliner Str 31 ☎ 920 39 70; fax 92 03 97 69 e info@miramar-frankfurt.de Ⓤ Hauptwache; Römer

Schlosshotel Kronberg
Queen Victoria's daughter had this luxurious castle built in 1894 near the Taunus Hills north-west of Frankfurt, and she resided here after the death of her husband, Emperor Frederick. The hotel's 24 single rooms, 27 doubles and 7 luxury suites are decked out with the original royal furniture. A walk around the exquisite parklands is the perfect end to the day after supper on the terrace.
✉ Hainstr 25, Kronberg ☎ 06173-701 01; fax 70 12 67 e www.schlosshotel-kronberg.de Ⓤ S4, Kronberg

Steigenberger Frankfurter Hof
(2, G6) Now part of the Steigenberger chain, the Frankfurter Hof has been around since 1876. The summer terrace out front has a dramatic close-up view of the Commerzbank tower across the square. Check out the hotel's wine and cigar shops.
✉ Am Kaiserplatz ☎ 215 02; fax 21 59 00 e infoline@frankfurter-hof.steigenberger.de; www.steigenberger.com Ⓤ Willy-Brandt-Platz

Martin Moos

Hotel Intercontinental

MID-RANGE

Gerbermühle
(1, G10) Feel like the landed gentry at this luxury guesthouse where Goethe used to court the daughter of a friend. The marble baths and elegant bedrooms (9 doubles) sweep you back in time until the babble of the gigantic beer garden outside beams you right back to the present.
✉ **Deutschherrnufer 105, Sachsenhausen ☎ 965 22 90; fax 96 52 29 28 🚇 S1/S8, Kaiserlei**

Hotel Alte Oper
(2, E4) Seven rooms adorned in a rich, warm decor right at the heart of the banking district; directly behind Deutsche Bank's shimmering twin towers, to be precise. It's the personal touch that makes this genteel hotel an overnight success.
✉ **Klüberstr 15 ☎ 72 61 62; fax 72 12 22 🚇 Alte Oper; Taunusanlage**

Hotel Am Dom
(3, C4) The bells, the bells! You could be mistaken for thinking you're at Notre Dame with the Dom's bells chiming in the day. Divas and artists tend to stay at this simple but elegant hotel.
✉ **Kannengiessergasse 3 ☎ 138 10 30; fax 28 32 37 🚇 Römer**

The memorable Hotel Robert Mayer

Martin Moos

Hotel Florentina
(2, F2) Little Italy in the Westend. One room with a view has a breathtaking rooftop terrace looking out towards the majestic Messeturm building.
✉ **Westendstr 23, Westend ☎ 974 03 70; fax 97 40 37 99 🚇 Westend**

Hotel Liebig (2, C3)
Sophia Loren would feel at home at this family-run hotel with its terracotta tones and Italian designs. The Palmengarten is a stone's throw away, and just to either side of the house are Gargantua and Erno's Bistro, 2 of Frankfurt's most reputed gourmet restaurants.
✉ **Liebigstr 45, Westend ☎ 72 75 51; fax 72 75 55 **e** hotelliebig@t-online.de 🚇 Westend**

Hotel Palmenhof
(2, D3) The house dates back to the late 19th century, and the furniture could be that old too. Each of the 46 rooms is individually decorated in period style, with some of the rooms at the back sporting a balcony.
✉ **Bockenheimer Landstr 89-91, Westend ☎ 753 00 60; fax 75 30 06 66 **e** hotel.palmenhof@t-online.de 🚇 Westend**

Hotel Robert Mayer
(4, B3) No two rooms are the same here, where local artists designed each of the 11 highly individual rooms that pay tribute to Mozart, Van Gogh and babies! (The lights in one room are in

the shape of giant dummies or pacifiers.)
✉ **Robert-Mayer-Str 44, Bockenheim ☎ 970 91 00; fax 97 09 10 10 Ⓜ Bockenheimer Warte**

Hotel Westend (2, F2) This period piece has 20 rooms on offer, and a charming collection of antique furniture. A Westend villa in the style the district's accustomed to, Hotel Westend is situated behind the banking district just a 10-minute walk from Opernplatz and 15 minutes from the centre of town.
✉ **Westendstr 15, Westend ☎ 74 67 02; fax 74 53 96 Ⓜ Westend**

Marriott Hotel (4, C4) You couldn't get closer to the trade fair if you tried! The night view of the Frankfurt skyline is spectacular from the top of this 44-floor monstrosity directly opposite the fair grounds.
✉ **Hamburger Allee 2-10, Bockenheim/Westend ☎ 795 50; fax 79 55 24 32 @ mhrs.fradt .res.mgr marriott.com; www.marriott.com Ⓜ Bockenheimer Warte 🚊 16,19, Messe**

Nizza Hotel (2, H4) This minimalist hotel is frequented by guest actors playing at the municipal theatre. Bathroom frescoes and Jugendstil furniture are just some of the artistic attractions. Breakfast on the rooftop terrace tops the bill.
✉ **Elbestr 10, Bahnhofsviertel ☎ 242 53 80; fax 24 25 38 30 Ⓜ Hauptbahnhof**

Charlotte Hindle

Marriott Hotel

Waldhotel Hensel's Felsenkeller (1, H11) The catacombs below the building have long passed into disuse, but the name (Felsenkeller) remains. There are 15 rooms at this family-run hotel on the edge of the Stadtwald in Oberrad, between Sachsenhausen and Offenbach. Oberrad is where the herbs for Frankfurter *Grüne Sosse* are grown, and you can be sure that the hotel restaurant serves a masterful helping.
✉ **Buchrainstr 95, Oberrad ☎ 65 20 86; fax 65 83 71 🚊 15, 16, Buchrainplatz**

Martin Moos

The old-world Hotel Palmenhof

BUDGET

12 Apostel (2, D9)
With 4 double rooms and 5 singles, there's room for more than 12 apostles at this inn, but only just! The old timber-framed house is a protected building, complete with original wall paintings. The bistro downstairs serves home-brew from the micro-brewery across the road (also called 12 Apostel).
✉ **Rosenberger Str 4**
☎ **28 03 88; fax 28 42 94** Ⓤ **Konstablerwache**

Haus der Jugend
(2, H10) Easily one of the best youth hostels in Germany, this sleeps almost 500, with a limited number of single and double rooms (DM54/44 per person, respectively). Guests usually sleep 4 or 8 to a room, and prices include sheets and breakfast. There's a TV room and cafeteria (lunches and dinners are DM8.90). Excellent wheelchair facilities. Bookings advisable during major trade fairs.
✉ **Deutschherrnufer 12, Sachsenhausen**
☎ **610 01 50; fax 61 00 15 99** **@** **jugendherberge_frankfurt@t-online.de; www.jugendherberge-frankfurt.de**
🚌 **30, 36, 46, Frankensteiner Platz**
🚊 **14**

Hotel Backer (2, E1)
Spartan, clean and cheap, with 20 rooms and communal showers on each floor, this hotel is right in the heart of the Westend, almost within earshot of the student district of Bockenheim.
✉ **Mendelssohnstr 92, Westend** ☎ **74 79 92; fax 74 79 00**
Ⓤ **Westend**

Hotel Bruns (2, E1)
This small guesthouse has 7 double rooms, and treats its guests to breakfast in bed! This has more to do with the fact that there's no breakfast room than a desire to peek behind closed doors, assures the kindly receptionist.
✉ **Mendelssohnstr 42, Westend** ☎ **74 88 96; fax 74 88 46**
Ⓤ **Westend**

Hotelschiff Peter Schlott (5, C6)
It may not be the Loveboat, but this anchored hotel has a romantic setting on the Main below the old town at Höchst. Breakfast is served on deck in summer.
✉ **Mainberg, Höchst**
☎ **300 46 43; fax 30 76 71** Ⓢ **S1/S2 Höchst**

Mercator (2, B10)
One tram stop from Konstablerwache, and a hop-skip-and-jump from Berger Strasse and Nordend nightspots, this place offers 32 en suite rooms, and free parking (space for 6 vehicles only, so reserve ahead). The excellent Exil restaurant is on the same street.
✉ **Mercatorstr 38, Nordend** ☎ **943 40 70; fax 49 02 17**
Ⓤ **Musterschule** 🚊 **12**

Pension Stella (1, C7)
Free parking is a cherished asset in Frankfurt, especially in the overpopulated Nordend, and one that Pension Stella offers its guests. Unfortunately there are only 4 rooms.
✉ **Frauensteinstr 8, Nordend** ☎ **55 40 26; fax 55 40 26**
Ⓤ **Adickes-/Nibelungenallee**

Camping Grounds

An even cheaper alternative is camping, and the following sites aren't that far from the action. Expect to pay about DM7-11 per adult, DM3.50-6 per child, DM5.50-6 per tent daily.

Campingplatz Mainkur (☎ 41 21 93), An der Mainkur, Fechenheim (1, C14) – a beautiful spot on the Main to the east of Frankfurt, Fechenheim old town is worth a closer look.

City Camp Frankfurt (☎ 57 03 32), An der Sandmühle 35, Heddernheim – situated to the north on the Nidda, this is just a triple-back somersault away from the outdoor pool at Eschersheim.

Lobby Camping (☎ 96 74 12 67), Niederräder Ufer, Niederrad (1, H4) – this volunteer initiative brings Frankfurt's homeless, long-term caravan residents and tourists together at a site down on the Main right next to the idyllic Licht- und Luftbad (p. 39).

facts for the visitor

Left to right: Martin Moos, Charlotte Hindle, Martin Moos

ARRIVAL & DEPARTURE

Frankfurt can be reached by air from virtually anywhere in the world, and by bus and train from the rest of Continental and eastern Europe. There are nonstop connections from the USA, Asia, Russia and most European cities. Contact air carriers and travel agents for off-season bargains and discount prices from no-frills airlines.

Air

Frankfurt Airport, Continental Europe's largest airport, is about 10km south-west of the city. It has 2 terminals, with Terminal 1 serving the German national carrier Lufthansa and its Star Alliance partners, Air Canada, Air New Zealand, ANA, Ansett Australia, Austrian Airlines, Lauda Air, SAS, Thai Airways, Tyrolean Airways, United and Varig.

Terminal 2 serves other airlines including Air France, British Airways, Cathay Pacific, Continental, JAL, KLM, Malaysia Airlines, Qantas and Swissair.

Each terminal has currency-exchange facilities, information counters and accommodation services. There are almost 100 travel agent counters in the airport's 5 halls, which are popular among Germans for bargain last-minute packages. Lockers are located in the Transit areas of Halls D and E (in Terminal 2) and Hall B (in Terminal 1).

Most major airlines have ticket offices in Frankfurt – consult the *Gelbe Seiten* telephone directory for addresses and phone numbers.

Information

Airport Information	☎ 69 00
Flight Information	☎ 69 03 05 11
Lufthansa	☎ 69 69 44 33
Car Park	☎ 69 01

Hotel Reservations
☎ 69 07 04 02 (Terminal 1, Hall B, near information counter 14, 7am-10pm); ☎ 69 06 16 62 (Terminal 2, Hall E, Level 2)

Airport Access

Train The fastest and cheapest route to central Frankfurt is via the S8 commuter train and selected suburban trains, which pass through the airport at least every 15 minutes between 5am and 12.30am, linking Terminal 1 with Frankfurt's Hauptbahnhof (main train station). The 10-minute ride costs DM5.90 one way. Tickets can be bought at machines near the escalators leading down to the platform. They can't be bought on the train, and passengers caught without a ticket are subject to a DM60 fine and will be ejected at the next stop. Follow the signs for *Bahnhof*. The terminals are linked by the Skyline, a 2-minute electric rail link.

Taxi A taxi to central Frankfurt costs around DM40. Taxi ranks are outside Arrivals at both terminals.

Bus

Bus travellers to Frankfurt arrive and depart from the bus depot to the left of the main entrance of Frankfurt/Main Hauptbahnhof, the main train station (2, H2). Deutsche Touring GmbH, a Deutsche Bahn subsidiary, is one of the largest operators. The main office is at Am Römerhof 17 (☎ 79 03 50; fax 790 32 19).

DTG travels to most eastern and western European countries and northern Africa. Its nationwide hotline is open Mon-Fri 9am-6pm, and Sat 9am-1pm (☎ 01805-25 02 54). DTG doesn't take telephone reservations. Buy tickets at the Deutsche Bahn Reiseservice Center at the Hauptbahnhof.

Train

With the new AIRail Terminal, Frankfurt Airport is connected to the national high-speed ICE rail network. A free bus shuttle service runs every few minutes between the AIRail Terminal and Terminal 2, which is linked to Terminal 1 by the Skyline (see Airport Access). Almost 90 long-distance trains stop at the AIRail Terminal daily, and it is also served by 4 of the main national routes: Berlin-Nuremberg, Hamburg-Stuttgart (both ICE), Hamburg-Basel and Dresden-Passau (both InterCity, or IC). In 2002, the airport will be linked to the ICE rail line under construction between Frankfurt and Cologne which should cut the 2hr journey to 45mins.

The rail service is operated by Deutsche Bahn AG (☎ 01805-99 66 33 for reservations and info; Ⓔ www.bahn.de (German only) for timetables and online reservations). The main train station, the Hauptbahnhof (2, H2), is just west of the city centre, and is Europe's busiest.

Passes & Discount Cards

BahnCard If you intend to travel extensively within Germany, this 1yr rail card is invaluable. Holders receive a 50% reduction on rail tickets countrywide, and can use the card for 13 months for the price of 12. A standard 2nd class card costs DM260, while 1st class costs DM520. For partners and spouses it's half-price. There are also reductions for families, children, students and senior citizens.

Schönes Wochenende Ticket For just DM35, up to 5 adults or 1 adult plus any number of children can travel on all suburban, commuter and subway trains countrywide as well as regional and city express trains from midnight on Sat or Sun to 2am 26hrs later. Perfect for groups going on weekend bicycle tours, though you will find that many others have the same idea, especially in summer. Bicycles are an extra DM6-9 each, although on some rail lines no surcharge applies.

Guten Abend Ticket With this pass you can travel anywhere within Germany between 7pm and 2am. For non-ICE trains, the pass costs DM59/99 for 2nd/1st class. For ICE trains it's DM69/109.

Stadtticket Deutsche Bahn has partnership agreements with most municipal train and bus services in Germany's large towns and cities. The Stadtticket (DM8-20 depending on the city) allows unlimited travel for up to 48hrs on trains, trams and buses in the city of destination. Purchase before departure.

Travel Documents

Passport

Your passport must be valid for at least the duration of your trip. EU citizens can use their identity cards or a passport that has been expired for up to 5 years.

Visa

Visas are not required by EU citizens, US and Canadian nationals, Australians and New Zealanders, some eastern European and South American nationals, and Korean and Japanese nationals staying less than 3 months and not planning to work. Citizens of some other countries in the Middle East, Africa and other parts of the world may require a visa. Contact the German embassy in the country of departure before leaving.

Return/Onward Ticket
A return or onward ticket may be required.

Customs

Like all EU nations, Germany has a 2-tier customs system: one for goods bought duty-free outside the EU, and one for goods bought in an EU country where taxes and duties have already been paid.

For goods purchased duty-free *outside* the EU, the limits are: 200 cigarettes, 100 cigarillos, 50 cigars or 250g of tobacco; 2L of still wine plus 1L of spirits over 22% or another 2L of wine (sparkling or other); 500g of coffee or 200g of freeze-dried coffee; 100g of tea or 40g of concentrate; 50g of perfume, 250cc of toilet water; and other duty-free goods (including cider and beer) to the value of DM115.

For goods bought in another EU country, and where taxes have been paid on them, allowances are more generous: 800 cigarettes, 200 cigars and 1kg of tobacco; 10L of spirits, 20L of fortified wines, 90L of wine (sparkling limited to 60L) and 110L of beer; and other goods to the value of DM350.

Sums of money of DM30,000 or more must be declared.

Landing, Departure & Passenger Taxes

All flights to Frankfurt attract additional landing, departure and passenger taxes. These vary depending on the country of destination or origin. For flights within Europe, typical taxes are around DM25 for landing tax, DM8 for departure tax, and DM18 for passenger tax.

GETTING AROUND

The Frankfurt transport system is easy to negotiate and works like clockwork, which makes getting round the city as easy as ordering a beer. Commuter trains *(S-Bahnen)*, trams *(Strassenbahnen)* and subway trains *(U-Bahnen)* operate more frequently than buses although the bus system is also very easy to use.

All public transport in the city is part of the Rhein-Main Verkehrsverbund (RMV), a network of trains, trams and buses linking the entire Rhine-Main region, roughly from Marburg to the north of Frankfurt, Aschaffenburg to the east, to the Bergstrasse south of Darmstadt, and the Rhineland region to the west. For RMV timetable information ring ☎ 21 32 33 22, Mon-Thurs 7am-3pm, Fri 7am-1pm. For fares, special requests or complaints ring ☎ 194 49 or ☎ 21 32 22 35, Mon-Fri 7am-3.30pm; or visit the Verkehrsinsel, the round glass structure at the Hauptwache (2, F7; ☎ 0180-235 14 51), Mon-Fri 9am-8pm, Sat 9am-4pm.

Fares & Tickets

A single RMV ticket for Frankfurt costs DM3 off-peak and DM3.60 in peak hour. Press *Einzelfahrt* Frankfurt for the quickest result. For a distance of up to 2km or 3 stops, press *Kurzstrecke*, which costs DM1.80 off-peak and DM2.10 in peak hour. Getting on a train, tram or bus without a valid ticket can result in a fine of DM60. Purchase tickets from automatic machines at most stations, and at outlets at Level B at Hauptwache and Konstablerwache, Level B at Bornheim Mitte underground, Level B at Bockenheimer Warte underground, and at the Verkehrsinsel at the Hauptwache.

While the integrated system is admirable, whoever conceived the ticketing machines must have had one applewine too many – they are complicated, to say the least. Each destination has a code number (Frankfurt is No 50), and place names are listed alphabetically. There are no zones as such. Instructions, complex as they are, are displayed in several languages, including English.

Travel Passes

One-day travel cards are the cheapest option and can be used for 24hrs on all RMV transport. A *Tageskarte* (day pass) costs DM8.20. A group day pass *Gruppenkarte* for up to 5 adults costs DM9, and DM6 for a group of children.

There are also weekly passes for DM30.60, monthly passes for DM107.50 and annual passes for DM1076 (the latter 2 are transferable, and pass-holders can take another adult for free after 7pm and at weekends).

S-Bahn & U-Bahn

The main form of transport is via the mostly underground S-Bahn and U-Bahn train lines. See the transport map for routes and stops.

Tram

The tram is a good way to view Frankfurt from above ground. The No 11 route runs from west to east between the towns of Höchst and Fechenheim. The No 12 runs from Sachsenhausen to Fechenheim. No 14 brings Bornheimers to Neu-Isenburg, while No 16 runs north to south-east from Ginnheim to the city limits at Offenbach. No 19 links Westbahnhof with the Waldstadion, taking in the trade fair area, Hauptbahnhof and Rennbahn horse-racing course, while No 21 links the south Main village of Schwanheim with the north-side Gallus area behind the Hauptbahnhof. See the transport map for routes and stops.

Night Bus

The RMV operates 4 night bus routes from the city centre to Höchst, Enkheim, Schwanheim, Fechenheim, Rödelheim, Berkersheim, Nordweststadt and Oberrad on Fri and Sat nights hourly between 1am and 5am. Buses depart from the Konstablerwache, and a surcharge of DM3 is levied on top of the regular fare. Disabled passengers and their escorts travel for free.

Taxi

There are plenty of taxi companies operating in Frankfurt, usually 24hrs. The large, beige-coloured Mercedes taxis with the rooftop sign are instantly recognisable. The main taxi stands are located at the Arrivals and Departure halls at the airport, outside the Hauptbahnhof, at Konstablerwache, Börsenstrasse and Merianplatz, the Alte Oper, and Darmstädter Landstrasse in Sachsenhausen. Fares are regulated, and taxis will take up to 4 passengers (for more than 4, ask for a *Grossraumtaxi*). The basic rate is DM3.80 with increments of 20Pf. Night-time fares are slightly higher. Passengers can negotiate fares for distances of more than 50km.

Taxis with an unlit sign can be hailed on the street. If you phone for a taxi, the switchboard will guarantee you'll be picked up within 6 minutes or else will tell you if it's going to be longer. Service may be slow during major trade fairs. If travelling early in the morning, it's best to book the night before. Drivers are well trained and are obliged to take the shortest route. Phone ☎ 23 00 01, 25 00 01, 23 00 33, 73 73 03 or 94 50 60 11.

Car & Motorcycle

Sometimes it seems there are more cars than people in Frankfurt, especially during rush hour, but it's not the worst city in the world to drive around. Parking, if you can find a legal space, is usually free outside the city centre, but you could drive around for 45 minutes and end up miles from your destination. Most car parks offer a reasonable overnight parking rate, but remove the car by 7am to avoid paying a day-time fortune. Traffic wardens prowl from 7am and will have offending vehicles removed expediently at up to DM250/day.

Road Rules

Vehicles drive on the right-hand side of the road. Wearing seat belts in the front and back is compulsory, and motorcyclists must always wear helmets. Accelerate when entering a motorway or *Autobahn*. Give way to your right on roads with no right-of-way signs (usually narrow residential streets). Bicycles have right of way at all junctions and crossings.

Speed limits are 50km/h in towns and 30km/h in residential areas, and up to 100km/h on national roads (B roads). There is a 120km/h limit on dual carriageways, and no limit on the motorway, although there is a recommended limit of 130km/h – you need good nerves and skill to venture onto the *Autobahn*.

Germans are good but often aggressive drivers, so don't be surprised if a headlight-flashing vehicle comes hurtling up behind you; you're probably hogging the outside lane, which is meant for overtaking. And don't stubbornly stay in the middle lane in 3-lane traffic; this slows down traffic flow and can cause a build-up. Beware of lorries and articulated trucks, which often make sudden unforewarned moves to overtake.

A number of motorway junctions are notorious for accidents and traffic jams, including the Frankfurter Kreuz west of the city towards the airport, and the A5 motorway between Frankfurt and Darmstadt, which has 4 lanes running in each direction at an average speed of 180km/h.

Rental

Car hire rates are competitive with rental companies charging DM320-420/week for the smallest cars (VW Polo, Golf). BahnCard holders (see the Train section earlier) receive special rail-and-drive discounts, and the main rental companies have counters at both Frankfurt Airport terminals and at the Deutsche Bahn Reiseservice Center at the Hauptbahnhof. Some also have offices in the city. The main rental companies are:

Alamo/National	☎ 69 07 23 60
Avis	☎ 69 03 26 31
Budget	☎ 69 07 44 40
Europcar	☎ 69 79 70
Hertz	☎ 69 59 32 44
Sixt	☎ 69 70 07 42

Driving Licence & Permit

Non-German residents may drive for up to a year on their local driver's licence. An International Driving Permit (IDP) is accepted but must be accompanied by your local permit.

Motoring Organisations
The main motoring organisation is the ADAC, which offers members a breakdown repair service; the distinctive yellow cars are a regular feature on motorways (☎ 01802-22 22 22 for repairs; ☎ 011 69 for traffic information). Nonmembers can join on the spot should they have a breakdown.

PRACTICAL INFORMATION

Climate & When to Go
Frankfurt is a year-round destination. The tourist season reaches its peak from June to August, while November to April are the quietest months. The weather in May, September and October is often better than in the 'summer' months June to August, which can be rainy and temperamental. The average temperature is around 10°C, but temperatures at the height of summer often soar well over 30°C. From November to February temperatures frequently slide below freezing point and storms are common.

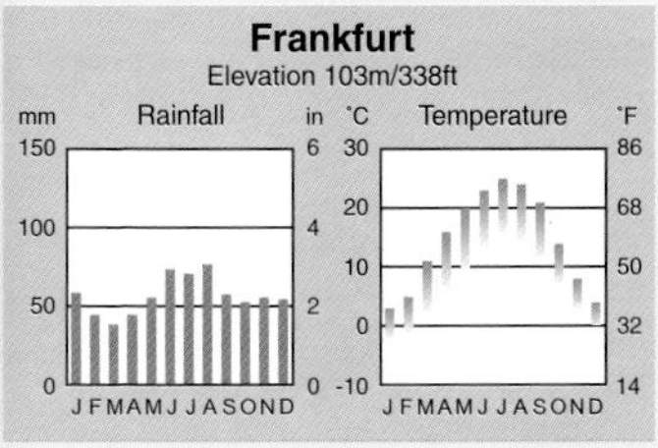

Tourist Information

Tourist Information Abroad
The German National Tourist Office (DZT, ⓔ www.deutschland-tourismus.de/e) has offices in the following countries:

Australia
(☎ 02-9267 8148, ⓔ gnto@germany.org.au) PO Box A 980, Sydney South 1235

Canada
Office National Allemand du Tourisme, (☎ 416-968 1570; fax 968 1986, ⓔ gntoyyc@d-z-t.com), 175 Bloor St East, North Tower, Suite 604, Toronto, Ontario M4W 3R8

UK
(☎ 020-7317 0908, ⓔ gntolon@d-z-t.com) PO Box 2695 London W1A 3TN

USA
(☎ 212-661 7200; fax 661 7174, ⓔ gntonyc@d-z-t.com) 122 East 42nd St, 52nd Floor, New York, NY 10168-0072

Local Tourist Information
The main tourist information offices are at Römerberg 27 (3, C2; ☎ 21 23 87 08; Mon-Fri 9.30am-5pm, Sat-Sun 9.30am-4pm), and at the Hauptbahnhof, near the car rental counters in the Deutsche Bahn Reiseservice Center (2, H2; ☎ 21 23 88 51/49; Mon-Fri 8am-9pm, Sat-Sun 9am-6pm). They organise tours and will reserve hotel accommodation. The Verkehrsinsel (the round glass structure) at the Hauptwache (2, F7; ☎ 0180-235 14 51; Mon-Fri 9am-8pm, Sat 9am-4pm) stocks endless brochures and tourist information, sells subway passes, and will advise you on transport and sightseeing.

Consulates
The following consulates are in Frankfurt:

Australia
(2, B4; ☎ 90 55 80; fax 90 55 81 09) Grüneburgweg 58-62, Westend

UK & Northern Ireland
(2, D3: ☎ 170 00 20; fax 72 95 5) Bockenheimer Landstr 42, Westend

USA
(2, B1; ☎ 753 50; fax 74 89 38) Siesmayerstr 21, Westend

Money

Currency

The Deutschmark (DM), which has been the currency of Germany throughout the postwar period, is set to disappear with the introduction of euro-denominated coins and notes on 1 January 2002. The Deutschmark is divided into 100 *Pfennige* (Pf). The 1Pf, 2Pf, 5Pf and 10Pf coins are copper or brass, and 50Pf, 1DM, 2DM and 5DM coins are silver. Notes (bills) come in DM5, DM10, DM20, DM50, DM100, DM200, DM500 and DM1000 denominations. Since its launch on 1 January 1999, the euro has been the currency for noncash transactions across the 11-member eurozone. €1 is equivalent to almost DM2 (DM1.956, to be precise).

Credit Cards

Visa and MasterCard are more widely accepted than American Express and Diners Club cards. Hotels usually accept credit cards but many shops and restaurants don't, and some will only accept EC bank-link cards (local cash cards). For lost cards contact:

American Express	☎ 97 97 10 00
Eurocard/MasterCard	☎ 79 33 19 10
Visa	☎ 0800 811 8440 (toll-free)
Diners	☎ 05921-861 234

Changing Money

Changing money shouldn't be a problem, and most large European retail banks offer free electronic cash facilities (ATMs) or only charge a minimal fee. At the airport there are a number of banks, mostly in Terminal 1, and currency exchange bureaus, mostly in Terminal 2. Opening times vary, but you should be able to find at least one open from 6am to 10pm. Ordinary banks will cash travellers cheques without charge.

Tipping

Restaurants	10-15%
Hairdressers	10%
Taxis	round up to nearest DM
Guides	10%
Porters	DM2 per bag

Discounts

Most attractions offer discounts to some or all of the following groups:

Children (check each venue for age limits)
People under 25 or 26 (with a youth card)
Students (with valid student ID)
Senior citizens
Disabled people
Family groups
Unemployed people

The Frankfurt Card offers a handy package of discounts including 50% off entry to 15 leading museums, the zoo and Palmengarten, 25-30% discount on tours and cruises, and free travel on all RMV public transport. The 1-day card costs DM12, the 2-day card DM19, and they're available at tourist information offices.

Travel Insurance

A policy covering theft, loss, medical expenses and compensation for cancellation or delays in your travel arrangements is highly recommended. If items are lost or stolen, make sure you get a police report straight away – otherwise your insurer might not pay up.

Opening Hours

Banks
Mon-Thurs 9am-6pm, Fri 9am-4pm; closed Sat-Sun and all statutory holidays

Offices
Mon-Thurs 8am-5/5.30pm, Fri 8am-2pm

Shops
Mon-Fri 8am-8pm, Sat 8am-4pm (but many open at 8.30-10am, and shops outside the centre may close earlier)

Public Holidays

1 Jan	New Year's Day
Late Mar/Apr	Good Friday & Easter Monday
1 May	Labour Day
May	Ascension (also Father's Day)
May/June	Whitsun Bank Holiday
May/June	Wäldchestag (half-day)
May/June	Corpus Christi
3 Oct	German Unification
25 & 26 Dec	Christmas & Boxing Day

Most banks and businesses are closed on public holidays. Museums and other attractions may close on Christmas and Boxing days. Venues normally closed on Sunday are also likely to close on bank holidays.

Time

Germany is on Central European Time (GMT/UTC plus 1hr). At noon in Frankfurt it's:

3am in Los Angeles
6am in New York
11am in London
1pm in Cape Town
9pm in Sydney
11pm in Auckland

From late March to late October it's GMT plus 2hrs, as clocks are turned 1hr forward for daylight saving.

Electricity

The standard voltage throughout Germany is 220V, 50Hz. Plugs have 2 round pins and adaptors to fit non-European-style plugs are available (though not widely).

Weights & Measures

Germany uses the metric system, though you will still hear supermarket staff referring to a pound of butter, by which they mean 500g.

Post

The main post office is on the ground floor of the Hertie Department Store, Zeil 90 (2, E9; open Mon-Fri 9.30am-8pm, Sat 9.30am-4pm). Others are at the Hauptbahnhof (2, H2; Mon-Fri 6.30am-9pm, Sat 8am-6pm, Sun 11am-6pm) and at Frankfurt Airport, Terminal 1, Hall B (5, C6; daily 7am-9pm).

For general postal inquiries and complaints call ☎ 01802-33 33 (12Pf/min).

Stamps are sold at post office counters and vending machines around the city, and at selected newsagents.

Postal Rates

A 20g standard-sized letter within Germany or the EU costs DM1.10; international surface and airmail costs DM2-3; postcards within Europe cost DM1; and international postcards cost DM2.

Telephone

Phones are either coin-operated or accept phonecards or credit cards. There's a wide range of local and international phonecards available. Lonely Planet's eKno Communication Card, specifically aimed at travellers, provides competitive international calls (avoid using it for local calls), messaging services and free email. For information on the service, visit the Web site at www.ekno.lonelyplanet.com.

The country code for Germany is ☎ 49, and the Frankfurt area code is ☎ 069.

Mobile Phones

Germany uses the GSM 900/1800 cellular phone system, compatible with the rest of Europe and Australia but not with the North American GSM 1900 or the totally different system in Japan (though some North Americans have GSM 1900/900 phones that do work here). If you have a GSM phone, check with your service provider about using it in Germany.

Useful Numbers

Directory Inquiries	☎ 1183
International Directory	☎ 11834
International Dialling Code	☎ 00
Operator Assistance	☎ 0010
Reverse-Charge (Collect)	☎ 0180 200 10 33

International Direct Dial Codes

Australia	☎ 61
Canada	☎ 1
Japan	☎ 81
New Zealand	☎ 64
South Africa	☎ 27
USA	☎ 1

Email/www

Internet Service Providers

Most major global ISPs, such as Compuserve (www.compuserve.com), AOL (www.aol.com) and IBM Net (www.ibm.net) have dial-in nodes throughout Europe; it's best to download a list of the dial-in numbers before you leave home.

If you access your Internet email account at home through a smaller ISP, your best option is either to open an account with a global ISP or to use Internet cafes. The main service provider in Germany is T-Online (www.t-online.de).

Internet Cafes

If you can't access the Internet from where you're staying, try an Internet cafe, although these are a dying breed in Frankfurt. The only one in the city centre is:

CybeRyder Cafe
(3, A2; ☎ 92 08 40 10) Töngesgasse 31, ⓔ www.cyberyder.de; open Mon-Sat 10am-11pm, Sun 3-11pm, it has around 15 terminals

Useful Sites

The Lonely Planet Web site (www.lonelyplanet.com) has speedy links to many German Web sites. Others to try include:

City of Frankfurt
www.frankfurt.de

MainCity Guide
www.maincity.de

German National Tourist Board
www.deutschland-tourismus.de/e

Frankfurt Map
www.stadtplan.net/brd/hessen/frankfurt_am_main

Frankfurt Restaurants
www.frankfurtrestaurants.com

Doing Business

Frankfurt is geared for the business traveller, but you won't find many services open to the general public. Photocopying, fax, computer and video-conferencing services are usually laid on by the many hotels and congress centres, and are reserved for guests and visitors. A good photocopying shop not far from the trade fair grounds is

KopierWerk (☎ 70 76 07 44), Adalbertstr 21a, in nearby Bockenheim. The main sources of information are the *Financial Times* (Mon-Sat) and the weekly *Economist*, *Business Week*, *Newsweek* and *Time* magazine.

The German American Chamber of Commerce has a Web site with useful links at www.gaccwest.org. The Australian Trade Commission is based at the Australian Consulate (see Consulates, earlier).

Newspapers & Magazines

Germany's only true national dailies are the tabloid *Bild Zeitung*, the country's biggest-selling newspaper, and its less sensational sister *Die Welt*. Otherwise, it's largely a regional affair, although the conservative *Frankfurter Allgemeine Zeitung* and Munich's liberal *Süddeutsche Zeitung* have a broad national coverage. These also vie with *Handelsblatt*, *Börsen-Zeitung* and newcomer *Financial Times Deutschland* for the business reader. The *Berliner Morgenpost* and *Der Tagesspiegel* have gained in prominence as political commentaries, while the *Frankfurter Rundschau* has a large local section but is read nationally for its quality left-wing voice. The Sunday newspapers are *Welt am Sonntag*, *Bild am Sonntag*, the FAZ's *Sonntagszeitung* and the financial tabloid *Euro am Sonntag*. *Der Spiegel* is the country's most influential weekly magazine.

UK dailies the *Guardian* and the *Financial Times* are both widely available, as are *Le Monde*, *Corriere della Sera*, *Wall Street Journal Europe*, *International Herald Tribune* and *USA Today*.

See p. 86 for magazines on the entertainment scene.

Radio

Frankfurt-based Hessischer Rundfunk or HR and Radio FFH are the mainstream local radio stations. The following stations can be received in the Frankfurt area:

American Forces Network (UKW 98.7)
  US military radio service

BBC World Service (FM 100.7)
  Global BBC service

HRXXL (90.4 MHz)
  Youth radio, lots of techno

HR1 (94.4 MHz)
  Information

HR2 (96.7 MHz)
  Culture and classical music

HR3 (89.3 MHz)
  Music and entertainment

HRSkyline (103.9 MHz)
  Lifestyle magazine from the top of the Main Tower

Radio X (97.1 MHz)
  Mostly techno and house music

TV

The public-service channels ARD and ZDF now compete with a growing number of private channels such as RTL, RTL2, Sat1, NTV, VOX and Phoenix. The local Hessischer Rundfunk operates the HR channel that can only be viewed in the state of Hesse and adjoining regions. BBC World, Eurosport, CNBC and CNN can also be received in certain cable areas and by satellite.

Photography & Video

Print and slide film are widely available, but trying to find a speedy development service is a bit more difficult. Super-Photo (2, E9; ☎ 91 39 86 52), Zeil 81, guarantees development in 1hr. Saturn Hansa (2, A14; ☎ 40 50 10), Berger Str

125-129, issues free film development coupons with every film purchase. Fotospezialist Martin Moog (2, E6; ☎ 13 37 94 26), Kaiserhofstr 13, stocks 120mm Ilford film.

Germany, like most of Europe and Australia, uses the PAL video system, which is incompatible with the American and Japanese NTSC system.

Health

Tap water is safe, though it contains high levels of calcium. Locals prefer the carbonated kind. No immunisations are needed to visit Germany.

Insurance & Medical Treatment

EU nationals can obtain free emergency medical treatment and subsidised dental care by submitting a valid E111 insurance form. For other nationalities, travel insurance is advisable.

Medical Services

Hospitals with 24hr accident and emergency departments include:

BG Berfusgenossenschaftliche Unfallklinik
(1, A10; ☎ 47 50) Friedberger Landstr 430, Bornheim

Bürgerhospital Frankfurt
(1, C7; ☎ 150 00) Nibelungenallee 37-41, Nordend

Universitätskliniken
(1, H5; ☎ 630 11) Theodor-Stern-Kai, Sachsenhausen

Dental Services

To find an emergency dentist phone the Zahnärztlicher Notdienst (☎ 660 72 71).

Pharmacies

Chemists can advise on minor ailments. Pharmacies *(Apotheken)* are the only outlets for medication, both prescription and nonprescription. They take turns to operate emergency weekend and after-hours services, and post details of the nearest on-duty chemist in their windows. Also call ☎ 11500 to find out about emergency pharmacy services. City pharmacies are usually open during shopping hours, Mon-Fri 8am-8pm and Sat 8am-4pm.

HIV/AIDS

The AIDS hotline (☎ 194 11) gives advice and support.

Toilets

Toilet facilities at the airport, Hauptbahnhof and public attractions are generally OK, and have facilities for disabled people and those with young children. There is usually a charge of 50Pf to use the facilities. There are excellent facilities in the Zeilgalerie mall's basement, at the centre of town.

Safety Concerns

Frankfurt is reasonably safe for a European city, but it's important to be alert at all times. Pickpockets are rife, especially around the Hauptbahnhof, and the Hauptwache and Konstablerwache subways. Drug addicts are generally more harmful to themselves than others, although there have been incidences of violence and addicts threatening passers-by with used syringes. Drug dealers have largely gone underground since a program to install fixer rooms for addicts was introduced in the 90s.

It is advisable to take the following precautions:

- When travelling by subway at night, choose a carriage with other people. Security personnel always travel in the front carriage after 9pm.

- Carry your passport, papers, tickets and money in a sturdy leather pouch on your belt or put them in your hotel safe.
- Don't leave valuables in your hotel room or in parked cars.
- Report thefts to the police and ask for a statement, or your travel insurance won't pay out.

Lost Property

Most items found on buses, trains etc end up at the Lost Property Office at the Hauptbahnhof (2, H2; ☎ 0202-35 24 42); or at the Allgemeines Fundbüro (1, G3; ☎ 21 24 27 38, 21 24 24 03 or 21 24 25 04), Ordnungsamt Frankfurt, Mainzer Landstr 321; or at the Stadtwerke Verkehrsgesellschaft (2, E7; ☎ 21 32 22 58), Hauptwache Passage, Level B. If you leave something in a taxi, call the taxi company.

Keeping Copies

Keep photocopies of important documents with you, separate from the originals, and leave a copy at home. You can also store details of documents in Lonely Planet's free online Travel Vault, password-protected and accessible worldwide. See www.ekno.lonelyplanet.com.

Emergency Numbers

Ring the police on ☎ 110 (free call) for crime-related incidents. In a medical or fire emergency phone ☎ 112 (free call). In case of poison phone ☎ 06131-192 40 (University Clinic Mainz). A children's emergency service can be alerted at ☎ 63 01 71 70.

Women Travellers

Women are rarely hassled, and can usually count on an incident-free stay. It's not unusual for women to enter bars and clubs on their own. Most car parks will have a women-only section usually marked *Frauenparkplätze*.

Information & Organisations

Pro Familia (☎ 59 92 86) gives advice on contraception and pregnancy. The Notruf für vergewaltigte Frauen (☎ 70 94 94) is a rape crisis hotline.

Gay & Lesbian Travellers

Homosexuality is widely accepted in Germany, especially in the former western states. Gay prostitution is legal and there are gay brothels in most cities. Berlin is the gay capital, but while the scene in Frankfurt is small it is nevertheless a very open one. It's mostly located around the city centre near the Konstablerwache. The age of homosexual consent is 16. Several groups are campaigning for a registered partnership law in Germany. Sexual orientation has been accepted as a grounds for political asylum. See 'Meet the Family' (p. 99) for details on where to get information on the Frankfurt scene.

Disabled Travellers

Disabled travellers should be able to make their way around Frankfurt with relative ease. The subway system has elevators as well as escalators, and ramps around the city aren't just an afterthought. Doorways on the most modern trams and on buses are practically level with the street, and are generously wide (older trams are impossible). Most new hotels, museums and tourist attractions are wheelchair accessible. Tourist information bureaus can give advice on how best to negotiate the city's amenities.

Language

Although German is a close relative of English, its complex grammar makes it a force to be reckoned with (fortunately, pronunciation is relatively straightforward). Frankfurters are proud of their local dialect, but the common language used in communication with non-locals is *Hochdeutsch* or High German (which all Germans learn at school). Any attempt to speak the language will be well received by the people you meet. For a more detailed guide, get a copy of Lonely Planet's *German phrasebook*.

You should note that the symbol **ß** represents the sound of a double-'s' in English.

Basics

Hello.	*Hallo/Guten Tag.*
Goodbye.	*Auf Wiedersehen.*
Bye.	*Tschüss.*
Yes.	*Ja.*
No.	*Nein.*
Maybe.	*Vielleicht.*
Please.	*Bitte.*
Thank you (very much).	*Danke (schön).*
Excuse me.	*Entschuldigung.*
I (don't) understand.	*Ich verstehe (nicht).*
Do you speak English?	*Sprechen Sie Englisch?*
How are you?	*Wie geht es Ihnen?*
I'm fine, thanks.	*Mir geht's gut, danke.*
What is your name?	*Wie heissen Sie?*
My name is ...	*Ich heisse ...*
Where are you from?	*Woher kommen Sie?*
I'm from ...	*Ich komme aus ...*
Do you have ...?	*Haben Sie ...?*
How much is it?	*Wieviel kostet es?*
It's fine – I'll take it.	*Das is gut – Das nehme ich.*

Getting Around

Where is ...?	*Wo ist ...?*
public toilet	*eine öffentliche Toilette*
post office	*ein Postamt*
tourist information office	*das Fremden verkehrsbüro*
What street is this?	*Wie heisst diese Strasse?*
How do I get to ...?	*Wie komme ich zu ...?*
(Go) straight ahead.	*(Gehen Sie) geradeaus.*
left/right	*links/rechts*

Health & Emergencies

Help!	*Hilfe!*
I'm sick.	*Ich bin krank.*
Call a doctor!	*Holen Sie einen Arzt!*
Please call the police!	*Rufen Sie bitte die Polizei!*

Time & Days

What time is it?	*Wie spät ist es?*
When?	*Wann?*
today	*heute*
yesterday	*gestern*
tomorrow	*morgen*
Monday	*Montag*
Tuesday	*Dienstag*
Wednesday	*Mittwoch*
Thursday	*Donnerstag*
Friday	*Freitag*
Saturday	*Samstag*
Sunday	*Sonntag*

Numbers

1	*eins*	7	*sieben*
2	*zwei/zwo*	8	*acht*
3	*drei*	9	*neun,*
4	*vier*	10	*zehn*
5	*fünf*	100	*hundert*
6	*sechs*	1000	*tausend*

Signs

Eingang/Einfahrt	Entrance
Ausgang/Ausfahrt	Exit
Auf/Geöffnet	Open
Zu/Geschlossen	Closed

Conversion Table

Clothing Sizes

Measurements approximate only; try before you buy.

Women's Clothing

Aust/NZ	8	10	12	14	16	18
Europe	36	38	40	42	44	46
Japan	5	7	9	11	13	15
UK	8	10	12	14	16	18
USA	6	8	10	12	14	16

Women's Shoes

Aust/NZ	5	6	7	8	9	10
Europe	35	36	37	38	39	40
France only	35	36	38	39	40	42
Japan	22	23	24	25	26	27
UK	3½	4½	5½	6½	7½	8½
USA	5	6	7	8	9	10

Men's Clothing

Aust/NZ	92	96	100	104	108	112
Europe	46	48	50	52	54	56
Japan	S		M	M		L
UK	35	36	37	38	39	40
USA	35	36	37	38	39	40

Men's Shirts (Collar Sizes)

Aust/NZ	38	39	40	41	42	43
Europe	38	39	40	41	42	43
Japan	38	39	40	41	42	43
UK	15	15½	16	16½	17	17½
USA	15	15½	16	16½	17	17½

Men's Shoes

Aust/NZ	7	8	9	10	11	12
Europe	41	42	43	44½	46	47
Japan	26	27	27.5	28	29	30
UK	7	8	9	10	11	12
USA	7½	8½	9½	10½	11½	12½

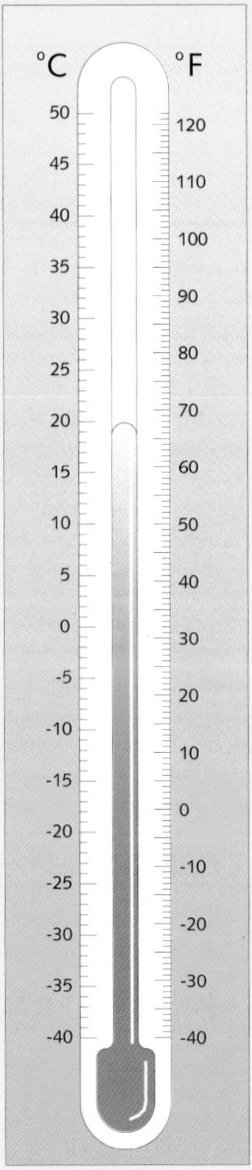

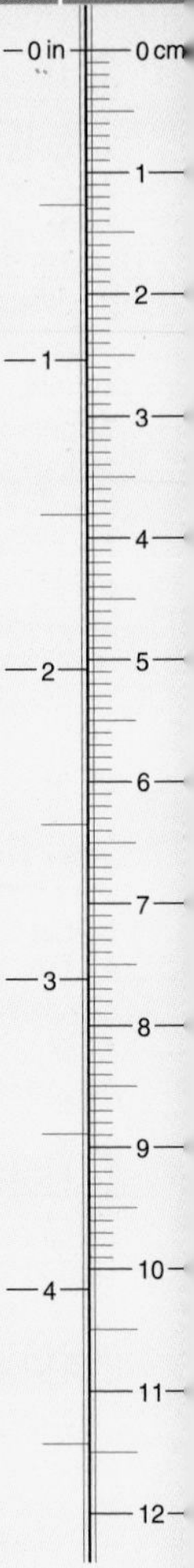

Weights & Measures

Length & Distance

1 inch = 2.54cm
1cm = 0.39 inches
1m = 3.3ft
1ft = 0.3m
1km = 0.62 miles
1 mile = 1.6km

Weight

1kg = 2.2lb
1lb = 0.45kg
1g = 0.04oz
1oz = 28g

Volume

1 litre = 0.26 US gallons
1 US gallon = 3.8 litres
1 litre = 0.22 imperial gallons
1 imperial gallon = 4.55 litres

THE AUTHOR

Angela Cullen

A committed European with unmistakable Irish roots, Angela came to Frankfurt in 1992 in search of the other half of her identity. Her Frankfurt-born mother had taken the more courageous step in the opposite direction almost 30 years earlier. Not to be outdone, Angela threw herself wholeheartedly into the task of converting Germans into Irish and Irish into Germans. A lucky Rhinelander called Harry (his mother calls him Harald) succumbed by marrying Angela in May 2000. The indomitable duo forced themselves to revisit favourite watering holes and seek out new ones in a research effort that left no Bembel unturned. Now they've crawled back into the Frankfurt woodwork to resume their regular existence – Angela works as a journalist at a financial news agency – in the city they've come to love, warts and all.

ABOUT THIS BOOK

Edited by Shelley Muir • Design by Andrew Weatherill • Layout by Vicki Beale • Maps by Charles Rawlings-Way • Publishing Manager Mary Neighbour • Cover design by Andrew Weatherill • Thanks to Arabella Bamber, Birgit Jordan, Brett Pascoe, Fiona Croyden, Gabrielle Green, Phil Weymouth, Quentin Frayne, Richard I'Anson and Tim Uden.

OTHER CONDENSED GUIDES

Other Lonely Planet Condensed guides include: *Amsterdam, California, Crete, Hong Kong (due January 2001), London, New York City, Paris* and *Sydney*.

ABOUT LONELY PLANET

The story begins with a classic travel adventure: Tony and Maureen Wheeler's 1972 journey across Europe and Asia to Australia. Useful information about the overland trail did not exist at that time, so Tony and Maureen published the first Lonely Planet guidebook to meet a growing need.

From a kitchen table, then from a tiny office in Melbourne, Australia, Lonely Planet has become the largest independent travel publisher in the world, an international company with offices in Melbourne, Oakland (USA), London (UK) and Paris (France).

Today there are over 400 titles, including travel guides, city maps, cycling guides, first time travel guides, healthy travel guides, travel atlases, diving guides, pictorial books, phrasebooks, restaurant guides, travel literature, walking guides and world food guides.

At Lonely Planet we believe that travellers can make a positive contribution to the countries they visit – if they respect their host communities and spend their money wisely. Since 1986 a percentage of the income from books has been donated to aid and human rights projects.

LONELY PLANET ONLINE

www.lonelyplanet.com or AOL keyword: lp
Lonely Planet's award-winning Web site has insider info on hundreds of destinations from Amsterdam to Zimbabwe, complete with interactive maps and colour photographs. You'll also find the latest travel news, recent reports from travellers on the road, guidebook upgrades and a lively bulletin board where you can meet fellow travellers, swap recommendations and seek advice.

PLANET TALK

Our FREE quarterly printed newsletter is full of tips from travellers and anecdotes from Lonely Planet authors. Every issue is packed with up-to-date travel news and advice, and includes a postcard from Lonely Planet co-founder Tony Wheeler, mail from travellers, a look at life on the road through the eyes of a Lonely Planet author, topical health advice, prizes for the best travel yarn, news about forthcoming Lonely Planet events and a complete list of Lonely Planet books and products.

To join our mailing list, email us at: go@lonelyplanet.co.uk (UK, Europe and Africa residents); info@lonelyplanet.com (North and South America residents); talk2us@lonelyplanet.com.au (the rest of the world); or contact any Lonely Planet office.

COMET

Our FREE monthly email newsletter brings you all the latest travel news, features, interviews, competitions, destination ideas, travellers' tips & tales, Q&As, raging debates and related links. Find out what's new on the Lonely Planet Web site and which books are about to hit the shelves.

Subscribe from your desktop: www.lonelyplanet.com/comet

LONELY PLANET OFFICES

Australia
PO Box 617, Hawthorn, Victoria 3122
☎ 03 9819 1877 fax 03 9819 6459
email: talk2us@lonelyplanet.com.au

USA
150 Linden St, Oakland, CA 94607
☎ 510 893 8555 TOLL FREE: 800 275 8555
fax 510 893 8572
email: info@lonelyplanet.com

UK
10a Spring Place, London NW5 3BH
☎ 020 7428 4800 fax 020 7428 4828
email: go@lonelyplanet.co.uk

France
1 rue du Dahomey, 75011 Paris
☎ 01 55 25 33 00 fax 01 55 25 33 01
email: bip@lonelyplanet.fr
minitel: 3615 lonelyplanet

World Wide Web: www.lonelyplanet.com or AOL keyword: lp
Lonely Planet Images: lpi@lonelyplanet.com.au

index

See separate indexes for Places to Eat (p. 126), Places to Stay (p. 127), Shops (p. 127) and Sights (p. 128, includes map references).

PLACES TO EAT